Considerations

COLIN WRIGHT

ASYM
METR
ICAL

Asymmetrical Press
Missoula, Montana

Published by Asymmetrical Press
Missoula, Montana.

Library of Congress Cataloging-In-Publication Data
Considerations / Colin Wright — 1st ed.
ISBN: 978-1-938793-80-6
eISBN: 978-1-938793-79-0
WC: 27,749
1. Philosophy. 2. Self-Help. 3. Considerations. 4. Personal Growth. 5.
Thoughts.

Cover design by Colin Wright
Formatted in beautiful Montana
Printed in the U.S.A.

Publisher info:
Website: www.asymmetrical.co
Email: howdy@asymmetrical.co
Twitter: @asympress

ASYM
METR
ICAL

ACKNOWLEDGEMENTS

A great big thanks to the folks who helped me whip this book into suitable shape for publication:

Chris Pinnock, Evie Socarras, Karin Gerson, Alasdair Martin, Tyler Constance, Chadwick Monkeymind, Tim Draws, Rivkah Greig, Eric Kenlin, Carol Brenneisen, Eric Evans, Kevin Grunert, James Andrews, Belle Betsy Orcullo, Alexandra Doligkeit, Mikael Suomela, Nikki Johnson, Gary Wimsett, and Shawn Mihalik.

Any typos or other mistakes are probably the result of me ignoring their damn good advice.

For all the amazing people who've showed me new perspectives over the years. It's because of you that I understand how malleable practical philosophy can be, and how wonderful it is that this is the case.

We should consider every day lost on which we have not danced at least once. And we should call every truth false which was not accompanied by at least one laugh.
—FRIEDRICH NIETZSCHE

You never really understand a person until you consider things from his point of view.
—HARPER LEE

Considerations

INCONSIDERATE

Few of us take the time to consider.

It's not that we're 'inconsiderate' in the sense that we're rude or brash or one of the other myriad associations we've tacked on to the word over the years, but we are often 'inconsiderate' in the sense that we act while seeing the world from only one standpoint: our own.

In many cases, this works just fine. It works so frequently that we become numb to the concept of stepping outside ourselves to find solutions that aren't immediately apparent; even when such solutions could help us solve the hefty problems we chisel away at our entire lives. By stepping a little to the left, a little to the right, or standing on our tip-toes, we may see something that allows us to crack the problem. But experience has taught us that we needn't make the effort. It has perhaps even led us to believe there are no other perspectives we can achieve; none worth straining to see, at least.

I would argue that a well-curated collection of perspectives is one of the most valuable assets a person can possess. Not only does such a collection add richness to everyday life and present solutions to problems we didn't know existed, it also provides the tools required to solve the big, heady, philosophical-and-hard-to-lock-down problems that we all encounter at some point in our lives. The 'what will make me happy?' questions and the 'how can I possibly go on after this horrible thing happened to me?' issues.

But not all perspectives are created equal, and each and every one has the potential to be valuable for one person, and worthless for another. A point of view that's *everything* to me might be ho-hum to you.

In this book, I've collected and presented some perspectives that have been incredibly valuable — in some cases life-changing — for me. This is not a how-to instructive tome, and you won't find the solutions to all of life's problems in its pages, but you may find some tools worth using, which you can apply to your own life, your own questions, your own problems, your own perspectives. You might also decide some or all of the ideas are worthy only of the mental scrap-bin.

Some of the ideas which are presented may seem provocative, or even offensive. Strive to work past any knee-jerk reactions, and ask yourself uncomfortable questions. Your answers may surprise you.

I don't ask that you take any of this at face value, or blindly trust that any of the concepts 'work.'

All I ask is that you consider them. Hold them in your hand, gauge their weight, and keep an open mind.

SELF-PERCEPTION

How much of what makes up 'you' is actually you?

That is to say, how much of your personality, your 'brand,' is authentic? How much of it is wishful thinking, or a version of yourself to which you aspire but haven't reached yet?

Most of us are made up of a little truth, and a little fiction. That fiction may be intentionally produced to cover our true selves with a protective veneer, but in many cases these pseudo-selves are neither laboriously constructed nor critically considered: they merely *are*.

This may be because we simply don't take the time to know who we *actually* are. 'Labeling theory' comes into play here, leading us to identify with others' perceptions of ourselves, subconsciously assuming other people will have a better idea of who we are than we do. In most cultures, too, it's not a priority to stop, take a deep breath, and question why we just did something; made one choice over another, or acted a certain way in response to a given stimulus.

Basing our self-perception on how others see us is just as one-sided as basing it on completely internal feedback. It's important to stop and ponder *why* we act as we do, and *why* we have certain habits and desires. But without combining that internal investigation with outside data, we're stuck with only half the information and fewer possibilities as to why things are the way they are. Alternatively, if we're able to look inward *and* gauge how others respond to us (and how we respond to them), we're far more likely to have an accurate view of ourselves, where we fit in the world, and why.

We often accept half-truths or fictions about ourselves because it's easier than accepting the potential mundaneness of fact-based reality.

There's a psychological condition called 'personal fable syndrome,' which essentially says that people see themselves as the heroes of their own storyline; as if the world revolves around them, their quests, and the details of their existence.

I would argue that if you *don't* see yourself as the hero of your own story, you're not giving yourself enough credit. Even the mundane can be interesting when put into the context of a larger quest. Even the most unheroic of personalities can grow and become the people they aspire to be, even if they have little reason to believe growth is a possibility.

Pretending that growth has taken place is much easier than actually growing. It's far easier to be known as the kind of person who helps the less-fortunate than to actually spend your money or time helping those who are less well-off than you. Similarly, it's less taxing to tell stories of adventure and intrigue than to live through the same stories.

Our brains are wonderful organs, and their ability to regulate our mood and self-perception is nothing short of amazing. But this same dynamo that gives us strength and power when we've actually accomplished something can be hot-wired to give us that same high when others perceive us as strong or powerful, even if we are neither of these things.

That means when others believe we are generous to those less-fortunate — and treat us like someone who is — we can get the same chemical reward from our brains as we would have were we *actually* generous in this way.

This is a powerful thing, but something of which to be wary. Though the immediate payoff can be worthwhile, it's a very simple matter to become addicted to faux self-perception, to the point that you never actually accomplish anything. As everyone else around you grows, you can stagnate, and eventually the guise will become transparent and render fewer and fewer results.

On the flip-side, it's possible to use this system to grow faster; to get a peek at what it might be like to be the kind of person you're striving to be. It may be possible, for instance, to present yourself as the type of person who *aspires* to help those less-fortunate than themselves, at which point you receive the social and mental rewards for growth, while simultaneously putting the pressure on yourself to actually grow. "Fake it 'til you make it" is another way of saying this, and though it doesn't work for everyone (especially those who fall into the aforementioned trap of addiction to unearned accolades), it can be a stimulant to keep on hand when you need a catalyst to work on positive growth efforts.

So long as your self- and public-perceptions are not presenting you as something you're not, such self-labeling can be a very positive, helpful tool. Don't pretend you're a doctor or try to convince others that you've seen or done something you haven't, but wear the demeanor of someone who's always learning, always growing, and make it clear what you're moving toward. In this way, the right labels can help you get where you want to be, rather than simply making you feel as if you're already there.

MONK

Consider the monk.

There are many variations on this theme, but the standard monk-concept is that life should be lived according to a code, and that in order to become the best possible version of oneself — or to achieve spiritual or intellectual fulfillment, or to avoid the chaos of the outside world, or to best serve a cause one believes in — one must adhere to strict guidelines, even sequestering oneself from the outside world completely in some cases, in order to step closer to one's goals.

Whatever it is you believe in, there's something simple and effective about this model: that in order to get closer to your goals, to make manifest whatever it is you hope to achieve in life, you must throw yourself at it, even to the point of ignoring other aspects of life. You must, in short, pull inward and search, think, learn, identify, find, ruminate, and grow. You must choose whether or not to take that which you believe seriously, and if you *do* decide to go that route, live your life accordingly.

There are plenty of reasons I'm not a monk, but I do think their practices are valuable in showing an extreme dedication to an ideal. Monastic practices can even be an example for those of us who aren't so certain about our calling, those who want to leave ourselves open to changing our minds about our calling, or those who don't really have a calling to begin with.

You can approach your personal growth in a monk-like fashion. You can take care of your bodily fundamentals — just enough food, water, and exercise to maintain your health — and spend the rest of your time, energy, and attention on that which you're pursuing; an ideal, idea, refinement of your own philosophy, or even just a good mental unspooling.

This sounds a lot like some flavors of meditation, but what I'm proposing is something a little more broad. Rather than focusing on a mantra or clearing your mind or chanting or even free-associating, decide on some kind of internal cause and allow yourself the time and environment to focus on it completely. That means removing (as much as possible) the cares of the physical world by eating just what you need to sustain your health, and working out in the same fashion. This means eschewing all other growth and work and productivity so that you might focus all your energy, all your pent-up ambition and potential to create, on one thing.

For a time, at least. The key difference between the pure version of the monk concept and what I'm proposing is that a monk may utilize such focus for his or her entire life, and I'm suggesting that you consider implementing it for one day, maybe two. A long weekend would be even better.

Eventually, it becomes possible to get into a monkish state of mind even when you have less time to focus. With practice, you don't need to commit as many hours to reap the same rewards, though setting aside more time doesn't hurt, if you can spare it.

It's all about allowing yourself to see what you're capable of, should you engage in extreme mono-tasking, beyond even the momentary lack of outward concerns you have during, say, a yoga class or a meditation session.

It's about becoming a monk for *something*, if only for a little while.

ABUNDANCE

We've all had ideas. Golden ones. Ideas so amazing that, if only we had the right audience, opportunity, lump-sum of startup-cash, or some other catalyst for fast-paced movement and widespread introduction, we'd be millionaires/cure cancer/have invented the world's best-tasting potato chip.

But ideas are cheap, and it's action that changes the world. You may have had a groundbreaking idea, but if you never act on it, humanity will never benefit from your brilliance. Or someone else will introduce something similar, and they'll drink your milkshake.

The problem with great ideas is that they feel very valuable, and as such are something we want to protect. Nurture. Care for and cuddle and treat with kid gloves. Part of why we do this is that we're very proud of ourselves when we have good ideas, part is that we don't want a competitor equipped with full financial-backing to steal it before we're ready to act, and part is that we're scared. Scared that the idea might not be as good as it seems in the variable-less vacuums of our brains. Scared that we might act on the ideas, present them to the world, and have them shot down. Scared that perhaps our secret gift for money-making/cancer-curing/potato-chip-flavoring isn't a gift at all, but just our own arrogance convincing us that we're something special, when we're not.

It's a legitimate fear, actually, that your idea might not be what it seems once thrown into the hectic hubbub of the real world, pulled from the soft, silent sanctity of your brain. And that's why you need to get that idea out into the world as quickly as possible.

Rather than protecting your ideas from the blights and blemishes of reality, you need to expose them to these imperfections as quickly as possible so they can mature and ripen in the correct environment. It's *possible* for a creature to survive in the rainforest after evolving in a coral reef, but it's not *likely*. Unless you want to keep your ideas stored away forever, unchallenged and unused, they'll eventually have to face the light of day, and it might as well be early on so they can adapt to the environment where they will spend their adulthood.

The best way to rid yourself of the notion that your idea will be shot down and you'll be left with nothing is to adopt an attitude of abundance.

This idea of yours, this stroke of genius, is not the only brilliant idea you'll ever have. If it doesn't work out, if the world doesn't appreciate it and love you for thinking it up, there will always be more opportunities. There will always be a new business model, cure-method, and flavor to discover.

This concept of abundance doesn't just apply to ideas. With any kind of creative work, if you hold back and hoard your projects, not only will you be denying others a glimpse of what you have to offer, you'll be denying yourself the potentially direction-changing feedback they might provide.

If you tell yourself this is all you'll ever have, then your mind will stop producing. Abundance breeds abundance, and scarcity breeds scarcity.

Produce more and think in terms of plenty and you'll always have more ideas. Allow yourself to learn from your mistakes and hone your craft, and you'll continue to generate a stream of new, ever-improving work.

TOLERATING

Talking through movies, impulsively tapping on tables, making off-color jokes, cutting people off mid-sentence; these are all things that are easy to miss if you do them, but which are *very* obvious to those around you. Someone may have even mentioned your annoying tendency at some point, but these types of habits are easy to dismiss in the moment as a one-time thing. "I don't ride the bumpers of other cars and complain when others do the same to me. Just that one time." Riiiiight.

Here's a question: are other people tolerating you?

Here's another: should you care if they are?

These questions are worth asking ourselves because they touch on two important points. They give us an excuse to see ourselves from the standpoint of others, while also helping us analyze what that gaze feels like; and whether or not it should impact how we behave.

The most obvious result of asking ourselves these questions might be recognizing that we regularly do something that's incredibly annoying to everyone but us.

When I was younger, I bit my nails like they were a four-star meal and I wanted to get my money's worth. It was something I never thought could be annoying to anyone else, but at some point a friend told me how much it bugged her and our group of friends, and I happened to be in the right frame of mind to pay attention to what she was saying (rather than discarding her words as a momentary thing, or an overreaction). Stepping back a little, I realized how gross the nail-biting probably seemed to others, and even realized that when I saw other people biting their nails it made me think they were nervous and weak-willed; unable to kick a silly habit.

Perspective gained, I stopped. Well, it took a few weeks of concentrated effort before I stopped completely, because the habit was so ingrained in my movements and reflexes. But I caught myself when I started nibbling and reprimanded myself when I didn't realize what I was up to until after a nail had been completely chewed through. Sure enough, the bad habit eventually disappeared.

There wasn't some immense difference in the way people treated me after I stopped biting my nails, but I did (strangely) begin to have people comment on what nice nails I had; they'd never noticed before. A very small change in my behavior, and a habit everyone around me had been tolerating was suddenly gone. My friends no longer had to put up with my thoughtless and annoying tendency.

Biting my nails didn't add value to my life, it was just a habit acquired during my childhood. Certainly the habit gave me a quick mental payoff of the kind that comes from performing any habitual act. But I was actually tearing up my fingers pretty badly, and the benefits of not biting my nails were much greater than the alternative.

There may be things others tolerate about you, however, that they *should* tolerate. Your political views, for one. Or your religious outlook. Your philosophies, in general. Your taste in music. So long as you're not pushing your preferences and beliefs on them, they shouldn't try to push theirs on you.

If someone makes you feel guilty for your views, they're the ones crossing the line, not you. There's nothing harmful in the sharing of information when it's asked for, but having someone else push their views on you because they don't agree with yours is *you* tolerating *them*, not the other way around.

A missionary preaching a belief system, dietary regimen, or workout routine to those who don't share their convictions and who didn't ask to be sermonized to isn't 'tolerant' — they're trying to force their beliefs on others. The people on the receiving end of that proselytizing are the tolerant ones, putting up with the constant conversion attempts.

If you find yourself the target of such a crusade, it could be worth telling your would-be converter that their evangelizing isn't appreciated; likely they're not being intentionally offensive, they just lack the perspective to recognize their actions could be construed that way. If they continue pushing, however, one needn't be tolerant of intolerance, or the attempts of some to enforce their moral code on the world through violence or coercion. Someone who refuses to stop pushing their worldview on you probably isn't someone you need in your life.

Be tolerant as often as possible, and surround yourself with people who are the same. Also be aware of who is tolerating *you*, and consider adjustments you might make that would improve your life, and the lives of those around you.

UPDATE

When was the last time you updated your beliefs?

It sounds like a strange question: after all, you believe what you believe because what you believe is true!

But is it?

It's a question many people never ask themselves because, frankly, it's far easier and more comfortable not to. The idea that we could be acting on faulty information, and maybe have done so for years, is a difficult pill to swallow. Even more difficult is the mind-bending process required to test what we *think* we know in order to gradually establish new, improved beliefs.

The first step is to acknowledge that you may believe things that are untrue. It's not an exaggeration to say that most people never make it past this step. Take a look around and note how many of your friends and family and coworkers still cleave to ideas about the world, about life, about themselves, which they learned or developed as children. From there, recognize that you may have ideas that are similarly incorrect or incomplete, and that there's no easy way to tell whether your 'big picture' is missing something significant. The same applies to everyone.

The next step is to separate yourself from your ideas. Part of why we cling to outdated notions is that they're *ours*, and that they belong to us; are one with us. We can't picture a world in which these potentially incorrect things are incorrect. It would be like growing up believing your cool uncle is a wonderful guy only to find out later in life that he's a serial killer. Even with an abundance of evidence, this would be a troublesome mental leap to make because he's your cool uncle; that's your jumping-off point for all other data you assess on the subject.

To extract yourself from a given belief, recognize that it's just one among many possibilities. Then take a deep breath and prepare yourself to rebound if your belief turns out to be incorrect or is brought into serious question. Because on that day, at the moment when you find out that some treasured way of seeing the world is not supported by fact — or is no longer supported by fact, as is often the case — it'll suck. And you'll feel like an ass. And you'll hate all the people who stumbled across this information before you did, because they might think they're smarter than you, and they're not.

Then exhale. It's all good. You can be smart and not know everything, and you can know a lot and still operate under the influence of flawed facts.

In order to determine what's factual and what's wishful thinking, it's best to derive information from multiple sources, and avoid heavily biased ones when possible (though it's arguably impossible to remove all bias from the process). In general, everyone has reasons to want you to believe one thing over another, and you'll need to identify sources of information that are supported by solid science, math, and mountains of historical evidence, rather than stern beliefs, gut feelings, emotional enthusiasm, or the like. Because while the latter is based on a biased point of view, the former is testable and changes as new data becomes available. That's the information you'll want to use when calibrating your beliefs.

You can, of course, believe whatever you want after going through this process. Just understand that there's a difference between beliefs built atop a foundation of factual evidence, and those perched astride junk information that's popular because it's shouted louder than other ideas or has the support of the majority.

There's never a bad time to reconsider what you know to be true. No belief should be safe from your investigation, and all should be regularly revisited. Consider conducting a regular internal review, to check and see if you've learned anything recently that might be in opposition to a belief you've held so long that it's become personal dogma.

Ideas about money, conspiracy theories, philosophies, spiritual beliefs, how society should operate, your own talents and skills and self-worth, are all worth revisiting from time-to-time. Only by establishing a habit of checking your own ideas can you be certain that at any given moment you're making decisions based on the most up-to-date set of personal beliefs available.

PRIORITIES

When I was a teenager, I promised myself I would be 'cool' until I died. And what that meant according to my teenage-self was that I would get older, sure, but I would continue to play games forever. All the games.

Video games, tabletop war games, collectible card games; I was a gamer kid, and I loved it. My lifestyle choices back in those days were spot-on for who I was and what I wanted out of life, and I made that promise to myself because I didn't want to get old and lame, like everyone else seemed to get. It was a mental letter written to my older self, pleading with future-me to avoid the pit traps that somehow made cool people boring and turned gamers into non-gamers.

Of course, it was only a few years after making that promise that I discovered art. And journalism. And girls. Three things that captured my attention and didn't let go until I found other new and interesting things with which to replace them (the girls thing stuck around, strangely).

Later came design, entrepreneurship, and publishing. As my passions evolved, so did my goals. I didn't want to become a championship gamer, I wanted to own my own gallery. No, I wanted to run a large design studio. No, I wanted to launch a tech startup and get rich with an IPO. No, I wanted to write books people would read and appreciate.

Changes in priorities emerged in tandem with my changes in interests. My hobbies evolved, and so did my intended progression within those hobbies.

There's nothing wrong with changing your priorities. You're not a sellout or a quitter if you decide not to be a gamer because there are other things in your life that are more important to you, now. A past version of yourself won't be disappointed if you choose to get married and have kids, rather than living the party lifestyle 24/7. I can say with absolute certainty that if he or she knew what you knew, he or she would do exactly the same thing.

Don't trust a younger, less experienced, far more ignorant version of yourself over your current iteration. Don't romanticize a set of priorities that perfectly framed a childhood version of you, but which don't fit your current dimensions. Don't be afraid to acknowledge when things are no longer important if they're no longer important. Similarly, don't be afraid to play the occasional game without needing to make it the center focus of your life; don't be afraid to have a drink, even if you don't plan to party like a rock star.

Live your life and allow your goals and priorities to grow as you grow. Otherwise you may find yourself spending all your time running toward a finish line you have no interest in crossing, for no better reason than you told yourself you would cross it someday.

THE DIFFERENCE

The only difference between a trash bag and a thousand-dollar carry-on is perception.

That's not the whole truth, of course — a more expensive bag is presumably better constructed, made of different materials, and allowed through an airport security checkpoint — but on a fundamental level, they're the same. They're both containers capable of holding and transporting things. Both conceal what they're carrying, and both are used by people to hold their possessions.

So where, then, does the perception of each bag come from? Why is it acceptable to carry a Tumi roller-bag, but a major *faux pas* to show up at a hotel with your spare clothing and toiletries in a black plastic trash bag?

The associations we have with each bag play a role. We've seen image after image of high-class travelers with their luggage, and as such know what to expect such a person to carry. Sometimes these images are in advertisements, movies, or TV shows. Sometimes they're described in literature, or shown in the news. Sometimes we see such people, luggage in tow, in real life. These types of bags are inextricably associated with this type of person, and that connection is personal, but spread culturally.

Likewise, someone carrying a trash bag implies associations of a less-flattering variety. The most common assumption is homelessness, because that's the primary cultural significance we attach to carrying our belongings in such a bag.

Consider that these associations extend beyond bags; we continuously make similar assumptions about people and objects and colors and ideas. Consider, too, that these assumptions are based on associations that may be faulty, or may benefit someone's interest (advertisers, for instance, might be trying to force positive associations with their product, or negative associations with a competitor's brand).

These knee-jerk responses can be very beneficial, and have a deeply rooted history in human society. Reflexive assumptions based on momentary, subconscious suppositions protect us by helping us avoid potentially dangerous situations — such as charging mastodons or pouncing saber-toothed tigers — without requiring us to first mull over every detail.

But today, in an age where our passive guesses are less about danger and more about consumeristic preference or ideological judgment calls, it's worth taking the time to determine which assumptions are legitimate and which are inherited from culture, past generations, or even our own (very limited anecdotal) experiences.

Testing our assumptions is an excellent way to see the potential in things and people we wouldn't otherwise stop to notice. A person with a black plastic trash bag could be a lot of things, and it's worth considering more than just your first impression if you intend to be an active participant in your environment, rather than just a passive experiencer.

CHANGE

If you could change anything about yourself, what would you change?

This can be a shockingly difficult question to answer, or even ask, because we're often torn between prevalent ideologies about how we perceive ourselves and whether it's too judgmental to want to change.

Some argue that wanting to change anything is not respecting the *real* you, and it's best to be happy with who and what you are now. I would argue that it's helpful to want to change things about yourself, but that it's best approached in a healthy way.

Unfortunately, some people conflate wanting to change with wanting to be more like someone else: wanting the figure of a famous model, for instance, or the athletic talents of a soccer star. This type of longing is a lost cause: you can't be that person (with their unique set of advantages and disadvantages, both inherited and earned) and trying to be them is a well-paved path to disappointment.

It's preferable to try to become a better version of yourself. You may not be able to have a supermodel's figure, but you can have an improved version of your own. You may not have a soccer star's athleticism, but you can work on your own endurance and speed and strength, resulting in a better you.

Rather than discounting yourself as a lost cause and wanting to be someone else, the trick is recognizing yourself as an excellent foundation upon which to build whatever you want. This way of thinking is more ideal because it recognizes your current amazingness while also giving you room to grow; to see what advantages you might have, and to discover how you might amplify them. It also helps you notice what disadvantages you possess, so that you can prioritize counterbalancing them.

Everyone has a different collection of advantages and disadvantages, be they biological, environmental, or social, and it's *most* beneficial for a person to consider their own improvement within their specific context. It would be silly of me to try to take the same career path as Oprah, because she and I are very different people coming from very different backgrounds. But that doesn't mean I can't aspire to a similar level of success. I just have to take my own, individual path in that direction.

After understanding this perspective — that it's okay to want to change, so long as it's an evolution of *you*, not you trying to become someone else — there are some natural follow-up questions.

If you want to change, and you know what you want to change, why haven't you? What actions have you taken today to get closer to realizing your goals? What's standing in the way of you getting there faster? And what are you willing to give up in order to become a better version of yourself?

Ask yourself these questions and do your best to answer them honestly. Then go. Do. Become the *you* that you're capable of being.

COST

Sometimes, I like to challenge myself to quantify how much it would cost to do certain unpleasant or dangerous things.

For example: how much would I need to be paid in order to eat a rotting, dead rat? How much to parachute off a skyscraper? How much to prostitute myself, or get a face tattoo, or wrestle a puma?

This method of quantification extends to other unpleasant, but less-dangerous or gag-inducing activities, as well. How much would I need to be paid to sit in an office doing work I'm not proud of for eight hours a day, five days a week? How much to put my name on a piece of work I believe to be of shoddy quality? How much to work with a client I can't stand?

How much would I need to be paid to date someone who didn't challenge or appreciate me? How much to attend a party I don't want to go to, or complete a conversation from which I derive nothing but boredom?

Adjusting the question: how much would it cost you to figure out what it would cost, then actually abide by those numbers?

I ask because for me, at least, there are some things I

wouldn't do for any amount of money, but most things have a price tag, even if it's astronomical.

I would gladly work a mind-numbingly boring job for several months, but only if I was paid a million dollars for doing so. After those months of boredom, I would have more resources with which to do any number of interesting things. The same is true for resources or rewards besides money: recognition or experience or whatever.

But if your price tag for working such a job is immense, and you're currently working such a job and not earning that sum, the question becomes: what would it cost you to act in accordance with this newfound standard? What would be the consequences — the quantifiable costs — of changing jobs? Of finding a new one with another company, or starting up your own business? What would be the risks, financial damage, and social baggage of such a move? And how does it compare to the gap between what you would need to be paid to make your current situation worthwhile and what you're *actually* being paid?

These are questions worth considering, and the answers, I think, are worth acting upon.

PERSONAL DEVELOPMENT

At what point does a focus on personal development become harmful to one's personal development?

It's an important question to ask, as the whole-hearted pursuit of something can become blinders, causing a driven person to lack the stable roundness of someone who is truly developed. In other words: single-minded focus on personal development can help one become, say, an impressive athlete who lacks any knowledge or ability beyond their chosen sport.

So where does one draw the line, to allow for focus without the cost of exclusion?

I don't think there's one right answer to this question. Some people focus on a task, reach a point of mastery, then move on to something else. Others work better when they have multiple, simultaneous concerns, leaning each body of knowledge against the others to achieve greater stability and higher heights.

I don't think it's the focus that's the issue here, because it's possible to be focused and still have a healthy respect for other fields and concerns. The real issue is 'personal development' evolving into 'this one thing is important and everything else is not.'

An example of this is people who don't read fiction because

they want to spend their time exclusively on growth-oriented activities.

It's not an unfair assumption to make, that fiction is for fun and entertainment, and nonfiction is work for serious people with goals to reach. Nonfiction delivers obvious teachable moments and bullet points. It feels like office work, sometimes, and plowing our way through the difficult parts gives us a sense of accomplishment.

Fiction, on the other hand, can seem a bit trivial in comparison. You read and interpret the text as you please. There are seldom bullet points, and the fictional scenarios are very different than the black-and-white facts you encounter in an office setting. The teachable moments are concealed inside metaphor and symbolism and dialogue. What could possibly be gained? Fiction is for the lazy, some might say. It's mind-candy. Fiction is for those who want something non-workish to do between bouts of work.

This opinion is very limiting, however, and misses many important points. Reading fiction has been shown to increase a person's mental performance for an extended period of time, and gives the reader a better sense of empathy, non-linear thinking, and numerous creativity-related benefits. In other words: because it's not an obvious solution for the personal development crowd, fiction is an oft-ignored tool that can help us develop faster.

Too much focus on one aspect of our lives can actually impede growth. Finding the point of balance — where you're able to push forward, full-steam-ahead, without missing all the interesting stuff that's flying past you along the way — is a goal worth accomplishing.

It's best to make sure you're not becoming so enveloped in one culture that you miss out on all the others. Same with book genres, or types of people you surround yourself with. To do so is to lack the perspective that will help you fully understand the things you want to appreciate.

It's also best not to push so hard in one direction that you actually harm yourself while trying to improve yourself (in addition to ignoring what's going on around you).

This is particularly noticeable with a person's health after they start a rigid fitness routine or a new diet. It's exciting to establish new habits — especially when those new habits flood you with happiness-inducing chemicals when you partake — but be careful not to push too far, too fast. A hacker who stays up several days in a row to build something amazing can die from lack of sleep, just as a bodybuilder who pushes too hard can snap their spine while lifting too much weight.

DEFAULT TO ACTION

I'm willing to bet you've done this before. You read about some topic (the Belgium UFO Wave, for example), and you're wondering, what exactly *is* the Belgium UFO Wave? You can infer a bit, and the context in which you encounter the phrase tells you a little, but you don't know anything more than this at the moment. You should look into it.

But then, for whatever reason, you're distracted from your task. Instead of hitting Wikipedia or Googling your way out of ignorance, you're distracted by a new kitten video or developing political scandal. Instead of hunting down information that would provide you with more data and greater context, which would file the information in your long-term memory, it stays a mystery. You don't even realize you've left a corner of human knowledge unexplored; that's how quickly the thread of potential enlightenment can disappear.

A better solution, in most cases, is to immediately follow through whenever possible. It would take only a few seconds to search for the Belgium UFO Wave, and a few more to scan the resulting information to see if it's worth investigating further. From there, you can either save the URL for future reading, or learn the basics at that moment. In this way, a small effort can yield a potentially large reward.

This is just one example, of course, and there are countless small acts that can improve our lives in an outsized way, if we'll only reach out and grab them. Take the initiative to act, rather than defaulting to casual inaction. Then determine whether turning that act into a habit is worth your time and energy.

One distinction between high-performers and those who tend to lurk around the middle or sub-average is that the former are willing to expend energy to pursue that which they're not told to pursue, and that which may be nothing (but could be something), and as a result have a wider range of opportunities and a larger, more far-reaching body of knowledge than those who choose not to explore.

Consider what you might accomplish with just a little more inclination to action, and the opportunities that might arise as a result of that investment. If there's a way to do something better, or to try something new, or to learn something mind-blowing, and it only requires a few minutes of active interest and activity, why not do it? Try defaulting to action for a while and see what happens.

EXTREMES

It's a relatively simple maneuver, hurling yourself from one side of a room to the other. It's even easier if you have some means of propulsion: a spring, bungie, or trampoline of some kind.

It's far more difficult to run toward that opposite wall, full-speed, and then stop yourself in the exact middle of the room. It's harder still to do so if you've been pushed by one of the aforementioned devices. Incredibly difficult.

Extremes of all flavors — ideological, dietary, professional, whatever — are also relatively simple matters. They're more challenging than standing still, but once you've got some momentum behind you, they're actually very straightforward. The bulk of the energy required is expended getting started, and all you have to do from that point onward is keep heading in the same direction.

Finding a balance by ascertaining where the middle is and then pulling yourself to a stop without falling down, however, is tricky. You have to get yourself moving, then slow yourself down and hope you stop somewhere near the middle, pulsing a bit here and there if you don't quite make it or if you go too far. It requires more meticulous control. You have to stay mentally 'on' the entire time, as well, lest you shoot past your goal or slow down before reaching it. You can't just hit the gas and turn your attention to something else.

Extremes are easy, balance is hard.

This doesn't mean that extremes are bad, but it does mean they tend to be blunt instruments, while balance is surgical and fine-tuned. Extreme diets and workout routines and optimization strategies and studying methods are large rocks, hurled at a challenge. More balanced approaches, with room for honing and recalibration and tweaking mid-stride, on the other hand, are sniper rifles fired from a mile away. Balanced approaches are less certain, but more elegant, and more effective if used correctly.

Yet, balanced approaches don't sell books or start belief systems. They're not sexy because they're not explosive or brutal. They're not slap-you-across-the-face impactful.

The type of effort required to achieve balance is quiet and reserved; uncertain, because the seeker of balance doesn't know where they'll end up. They don't know, because they can't find their center point until they've seen a little of both ends and everything in between. Balance appears humble when compared to the brash certitude of extremism.

It's easier to find balance if you're looking for it from the get-go, but take a look at your beliefs and pursuits and see if any of them could use more refining and meticulous management, and a little less grunting and posturing. You'll be happier with the results, and you might even prevent a hernia (literally or figuratively).

DIFFICULT QUESTIONS

So here's a tough question to answer: is anything worth dying for?

Pop culture wisdom says, yes, of course. Your family, or a bystander. Your fellow soldiers or your political leaders or a child who's about to be hit by a bus.

But social expectations aside, *is* anything worth dying for? Consider that if you're dead, you won't reap any of the benefits of dying bravely. You won't be thanked or glamorized. Your country may thank you, or the child's family may thank you, but those thanks will fall upon deaf ears. Those you leave behind — your loved ones — may benefit, but they also lose you, so it's debatable as to whether it's a good tradeoff for anyone involved.

I think if you asked most people whether anything was worth dying for, many would say yes, of course. They would die for their significant other or ideology or some philosophical cause that's near and dear to them.

But if they did, in fact, throw themselves in front of a bullet for their love of democracy or the Denver Broncos or an endangered pigeon, I wonder how many, in those last moments, would regret their actions? Would realize that their sacrifice might not mean as much as it seemed mere seconds before?

33

Would they, in that moment, think about what it means to die and what death means for consciousness and the ability to love or appreciate or support or protect?

Does the world go on when you're not there to perceive it?

And if you don't know (science doesn't, yet), does that matter? Would it be worse to have the opportunity to die for something and not take it? Would it be better to not *be*, than to exist with that kind of regret?

These are not questions with a single answer, or perhaps any answer. I would guess most people struggle with such things if and when they think about them, and that's precisely why most will never take the time to mull over such difficult thoughts.

I propose these are exactly the questions that need to be considered, however, because there's a chance — just a chance, but that's better than nothing — that doing so ahead of time will allow you to make the right choice, for you, if you ever have to.

Pondering unthinkable questions is what allows us to come up with answers that matter, and allows us to save a life or decide not to, fully aware of the repercussions of both decisions. Difficult questions shouldn't be avoided, because answers arrived at easily are more likely to be incorrect or incomplete.

LISTS

We all have a list of things we'd like to accomplish before we die, whether it's scrawled on paper or some digital medium, or maintained mentally in an ever-shifting bit of brain matter.

It's wonderful seeing people post their 'bucket lists' online and add new things to them. It makes us aware of our transient nature to plan for what we'd like to do before the end arrives, and anything that allows us to embrace the finite *and* still have fun is a positive in my book.

That being said, these lists have become a popular item to include on one's blog or social media account (there are even dedicated social networks expressly for bucket list building and maintenance), and consequently they're often a form of social proof rather than a collection of intended life accomplishments.

The result is that rather than cataloging goals we actually have aspirations to achieve, we list things that are very impressive and intense-sounding for the sake of being associated with those types of activities. We might add scaling a mountain, though we have no interest in scaling anything, for example. We list things that support the idea or image of ourselves we'd like to convey.

This, of course, destroys the whole purpose of a bucket list. What should be an actual, actionable checklist of things you want to systematically experience or do, instead becomes a 'favorite intentions' list; not meant to represent goals, but rather things that you like. Things you approve of. It's the equivalent of having a list of favorite TV shows, but instead of CSI or Dexter, you have skydiving and eating kangaroo meat.

If you actually intend to do those things, and if you believe they will truly bring you pleasure, excellent! You're on the right track. My aforementioned concerns don't apply.

If your list is heavy with the goals of others, however, or if you can't actually see yourself doing some of the things you listed, take the time to start fresh and be more truthful about your objectives. If you're a cooking aficionado, instead of listing 'Climb Mt. Kilimanjaro,' maybe say 'Learn to cook a mean pad thai.' If you prefer staying put to traveling, maybe leave 'Visit the Eiffel Tower' off your list, and instead decide to 'Read every story ever written by Isaac Asimov.'

In short, make sure your goals are for *you*, not for others' perception of you. This applies to all goals, not just those on some sort of bucket list.

If you want to impress strangers on the internet, take a few decent selfies and write an amusing blog post every once in a while. If you want to live a good life, figure out what it is that actually makes you happy and do more of that.

DEBT

What would you do if you had no debt?

For some, this question is easy to answer because they've managed to avoid accruing any debt, or have already paid theirs off. Being debt-free is not common — most of us have some kind of debt, be it school- or home- or gambling-related — but some people manage to get there.

I remember when I got out of debt, having just paid off my final $30k in student loans and $5k in car payments. It was such a liberating feeling; I was suddenly untethered from a boulder-like weight and anything was possible. I realized that if I killed off some of my other recurring expenses I could live on very, very little money: a thought that opened even more doors.

But until debt is paid, you owe someone something, and that's a feeling most of us don't like, even if it's not a conscious burden most of the time. It makes every little stress a little more stressful, and every little problem all the more problematic. You can be living the high-life, but if you're in debt, it can feel like everything you have may come crashing down around you at any moment.

What do you think would happen, if everyone's debt was eliminated?

It's an idea that's been proposed in different ways and in different forums numerous times in the past, and though I doubt it will ever happen, try to imagine the repercussions of such a massive act. There are countries whose debts to private interests and other countries keep them on the precipice. There are politicians ensnared by the debts they owe lobbyists and businesses and each other. On a more localized level, generations of people have made career decisions based on money so that they'll be capable of paying off school debt, or can afford to pay down their home loan.

It's safe to assume many people would immediately go back into the red, should their existing debt disappear, as the desire for rewards *now* can outweigh the benefits of waiting, for some.

But for others — people who would find themselves with a sense of freedom previously unexperienced in their adult lives — I think becoming debt-free would be revelatory. I think it would give them the chance to reassess and make better choices, knowing what they know now, compared to what they knew when the banks were first throwing plastic at them as they came of legal age.

I think we'd see most people acting rationally about money and their money-making activities, perhaps for the first time in their lives, because they've never had the combination of experience-gained responsibility and a blank slate before.

Without debt, we might all be new people.

Of course, we may never know what would happen on a large scale, if everyone's debt was eliminated. It's unlikely that the Forces That Be would consider this a worthwhile move, because there's always someone benefitting from keeping others under their thumb.

On a smaller scale, though, it's possible to see these changes and notice these differences. To take what you've learned and apply it as you see fit. Focus on paying down debt — it doesn't take as long as you'd think, though it's not easy by any means — and reach that goal. See for yourself who you are without it.

Would you be the type of person to fall back into the same, cozy, comfortable habit of instant gratification at the expense of personal freedom? Or would you learn from past experiences and live within your means? Would you figure out what your means are, and what your needs are, and adjust your lifestyle accordingly?

There's only one way to know for sure.

LENSES

Consider that all of your beliefs originated somewhere. You didn't emerge from the womb supporting a particular sports team, believing in a specific economic system, or subscribing to a given faith. All of these things came later.

It can be difficult to trace the development of our beliefs, but some common sources are our parents, our childhood friends, the media we consumed growing up (TV, radio, books, newspapers), advertisers, and formal education.

As time passes, more influencers are added, and the chance that our ideas have come from our own interpretations of events increases, though we can still only interpret life events based on our existing knowledge and opinions, so even these self-derived concepts tend to be skewed by the biases of others, not just our own.

This is not to say we should ignore the opinions of others, or defend ourselves against academia or brands or the ideas our parents hold dear. The point is that we need to be aware that our view of world is filtered through overlapping lenses made up of different influences. These lenses are so effective that you and I could see the exact same car accident and perceive it in different ways. Or the same sky. Or the same piece of artwork. Or read the same piece of literature. Or encounter the same philosophy or idea.

This means that all those other people in the world who believe differently than us are not idiots or uninformed or evil, they're simply viewing the world through a different combination of overlapping lenses. Their view is just as real to them as your view is to you, and any other way of seeing the world — including yours — is as difficult for them to comprehend as theirs is for you.

What a liberating concept! This means we needn't focus on converting others to our way of seeing things, because the very concept of conversion is riddled with flaws. You can't expose another person to your worldview and just expect them to see it the same way you do, because their perception is inherently different than yours; just as rich with influences as your own.

I say this is liberating because it means that rather than feeling an incessant drive to proselytize our point of view, we can simply make available the information we find to be important and consider our work complete. I cannot change the way you see the world, fundamentally, any more than you could forcibly change my perspective. But if I put some information out there, or perhaps a question for you to consider, or a thought experiment, you can take that question or idea or exercise and run with it; pass it through your filters and perhaps arrive at a destination similar to mine.

Or not. The only way you can experience something is from the standpoint of someone with your exact background and collection of influences. That you receive the same information as me and arrive at a different conclusion is only natural.

Imagine a world where this concept shaped everyone's approach to conveying information and sharing ideas. Instead of attempting to convert other people, we would make data available and share it in the cleanest and most intuitive way possible. We could then follow up with more information if the consumer wishes it. It would be the equivalent of saying, "Here's what you need to know about what I believe. I'm available for questions if there are any you'd like to ask. Good day to you."

If this method of sharing ideas became widespread, the field of advertising and philosophy of consumption would change overnight, and most of us would be happier not just with ourselves and our own beliefs, but with others and their beliefs, as well.

Conflicts over differing views and values would be a thing of the past, because we could acknowledge each other's truth: that every one of us is building the best life we possibly can for ourselves. We're all just working from different sets of instructions.

HABITS

Creating and maintaining habits is a choice. We adopt habits without thinking, but we can also (sometimes with great difficulty) change the course of these habits, end them completely, or start new ones. It's one of the many superpowers we have as human beings.

What good is an unused superpower? When properly wrangled, habits forged by willpower are a pathway to new skills, a healthier body, and an optimally functioning mind — a better *you*. Integrating dietary changes, exercise, brain-calibrating activities like meditation, and regular training of skill-based abilities (like writing or painting or dodgeball or whatever) can make you a better version of yourself, without changing the unique core that makes you who you are. How great is that?

Habits can also be a net-negative for your life, however. Habitual over-drinking, smoking, or drug-use can destroy your health. Habitual sloth and mind-numbing activities can do the same for your physical fitness and mental state. There are chemical reasons why it's difficult to quit bad habits, but that doesn't mean you *can't* break them. It just means it takes hard work and patience to transmute bad habits into something less harmful, so it's probably a good idea not to pick up negative habits to begin with.

So here's a question: given the option, why not develop positive habits rather than negative ones?

I think the gut response for many of us is that we didn't realize we'd picked up a bad habit until it was too late to easily kill it off, but I call shenanigans on this excuse. It implies we *can't* pay closer attention and negate such habits before they become an issue moving forward, and that's simply not true.

Yes, it can be hard to catch yourself biting your nails, but over time, with some effort and willpower invested, you'll notice and stop yourself, pre-bite. Eventually the reflex to nibble will disappear, and you'll engage in that habit less frequently. Alcoholism is a 'disease' in that there's a chemical component and some are more prone to it than others, but that doesn't mean an alcoholic is helpless to stop drinking. It just means doing so will be more difficult for them than for someone who's less prone, chemically, genetically, and environmentally to substance abuse.

Beyond catching and ending bad habits, though, how about starting new, positive habits? This process looks different for everyone, but most of the truly happy and successful people I know are masters of first deciding what changes they want to see in their lives, and then immediately working to create habits that will help them make those changes manifest.

After all, a habit is just a repetitive act you do without thinking, and if you can kindle positive, mindless acts you perform without having to struggle through soul-crushing doubt and habitual inaction, wouldn't that be worth a little bit of up-front investment of your time and effort? Wouldn't it be worth figuring out what habits you can seamlessly fit into your life, without sacrificing too much in the tradeoff?

I say yes. And I say the only real question, once this habit-forming ability has been accepted, is this: what habits would you like to have?

And a followup: why not start a positive habit right now?

DEFINITION OF GROWTH

Each of us has a different definition of growth.

For some, it's all about money. In the post-Industrial Revolution world, money has become the default unit of measurement for growth and success and personal evolution; self-worth. "I'm making twice as much as I was three years ago," is one way to measure growth using this metric.

For others, growth is a less quantifiable development. Becoming more knowledgable, for example, or more well-known within your field can be considered growth. Sometimes there are awards or other accolades that indicate the same. But there's no commonly accepted ranking system, and all a person has is their own interpretation of movement; their own ideas about how much they've grown.

Without an objective unit of measurement, it can seem impossible to empirically determine if the changes you've made in your life — the choices you've made professionally, personally, health- and mind-wise — have been the right ones. It can be hard to tell if they've resulted in growth, recession, or stagnation.

It's harder still to measure your personal growth if your unit of measurement changes. Years ago, I measured my success based on how much money I earned each year. Today, I measure it based on a combination of the amount of personal freedom I enjoy, the level of happiness I experience, the amount of value I produce, and numerous other things that are difficult to express and even more difficult to measure.

So how do you grow if you don't know how to grow? Especially if you don't know what growth looks like?

How do you know if growth has occurred in the first place? How do you measure what can't be easily measured or even reliably identified?

It could be that everyone has their own metric, and therefore we don't need to identify an overarching unit of measurement for personal growth, because it doesn't exist.

It could be that such growth can't be measured at all. Maybe, even on an individual level, trying to measure growth outside the numerical is a fool's errand. Maybe focusing on growth — or the measurement of it — is missing the point of living well. Maybe the entire process is one unit of a much larger system, and trying to break it up into pieces would be like trying to measure atoms without first developing millimeters: maybe most of us aren't capable of measuring such things yet.

Or maybe I'm wrong and comparisons are possible. Maybe each person can work out an accurate conversion table for their happiness, comparing money earned to time spent, happiness felt to books read, knowledge gained to social status attained. Maybe seeking and finding that kind of ratio-driven system is just what you need and will help you achieve the best life possible, no matter what it is you hope to accomplish

But you'll never know one way or the other if you never stop to ascertain what you're reaching for, and why. Asking yourself these questions — addressing all the 'maybe's — and defining

47

what growth means to you, is the only way to calibrate toward fulfillment, personal evolution, and ultimately, happiness.

OUTRAGE

Outrage is sexy. It sells newspapers and attracts online clicks. If you want to raise a ruckus, get outraged, because people go gaga over people going gaga.

Of course, that's all the value one can get from outrage. Although entertaining to watch and speculate over and gossip about, outrage very, *very* seldom changes anything, and can even make a bad situation worse by injecting anger into the mix.

On a personal level, outrage makes us feel superior. By becoming indignant, we're drawing a line in the sand and declaring ourselves to be on the right side of a given issue. We're saying, "How horrible this situation is, and how capable I am of declaring right and wrong, and passing judgment on those involved!"

Whether we actually happen to be right or wrong is irrelevant, because the sense of injustice we revel in is actually a self-esteem boost, gained by climbing atop rabble and rubble. It makes us feel taller to indignantly puff ourselves up with outrage.

The share-rate of rage-inducing news can be attributed to the flood of 'hurts so good' chemicals that accompany righteous anger. Getting hooked on this feeling is all too common, and causes us to seek it out. The need to be angry or upset in order to feel good is a sad state of affairs. Look around: there's no shortage of business models predicated on saturating people with these chemicals, keeping them hooked on an anger-induced high.

To avoid this type of addiction, it's best to avoid delving into scandals and fabricated, bias-heavy news items and storylines. Instead, decide where and how you can actually make a difference.

This move is guaranteed to pour water over the rage-high we might otherwise get hooked on, because it requires us to think rationally — not emotionally — and requires us to determine which problems we will participate in solving and which are just fun to get upset about.

If you want to be involved in something scandalous, *do something* other than sitting around and seething, while spreading the same venom to others.

Anger without action leaves us feeling as though we've accomplished something when we haven't. This results in fewer solutions, not more, because the desire to solve the problem is washed away by the feeling of satisfaction we get from being incensed. Resentment without an effort to rectify accomplishes exactly nothing, and makes us part of the problem we're so angry about.

In short: if you're not willing to lift a finger to solve a problem, you've lost the right to complain about it. By complaining more selectively, we'll spend more time solving problems and sharing solutions, and less time perpetuating outrage-addiction.

DECISIONS

Some of the most efficient solar panel arrays in the world are monitored and controlled by software that chooses the optimal position for each panel, ensuring that the maximum amount of energy is harvested for the smallest number of resources used.

How does the array do this?

Data, mostly. And algorithms that convert that data into high-yield action.

This is why software development is such a valuable skill set: if you're able to build a 'brain' that utilizes data better than the brain someone else built, you've potentially saved millions of dollars. Or collected twice as much energy.

The data part of this equation is vital. Without knowing about weather patterns (present, predicted, and historical), the panels cannot decide how best to align themselves with the minimum amount of energy expended. In addition, if these panels don't keep close tabs on such data, while also collecting information about when they need maintenance and upgrades, they can't determine the best methods and routines for ideal output and upkeep.

In short, the most optimal software is both clever and informed. The same can be said for the optimal human mind.

Human beings are pretty amazing beasts. Our brains are phenomenally complex organs, and are capable of ridiculous feats of unbounded awesomeness.

Without proper input, however, these amazing brains of ours are never pushed to achieve their full potential. They aren't working at full capacity because they haven't been fed the knowledge (data) to function properly.

A data-starved brain makes poorer decisions than a data-saturated brain. Being data-starved also prevents a brain from optimally maintaining the hardware it's attached to (the body), and is not as capable of developing upgrades (innovation and creativity).

In short, unless you use your brain, tax it a little, and expose it to new things — new experiences, new information, new ideas — it may as well be another kidney for all the good it's doing you. It'll keep you from tipping over or petting a lion, but not much else. Such wasted potential.

The brain-as-computer metaphor is an imperfect one, but it's useful for understanding what we need and why. And how those inputs — all that knowledge and those experiences — impact the decisions we make, the lives we live, and the happiness we enjoy.

BRANDING

A brand is the collection of sights, sounds, smells, styles, words, and other attributes associated with you as an entity.

Which is a fancy way of saying your brand is the perception of you as a complete person. Your personality, your work, the way you interact with others, your taste in clothing and food, the way you carry yourself — all of these elements aggregate into a single persona.

If this persona is clearly enunciated — something that's easy to understand, tell others about, and relate to — it can help you communicate the important things about yourself, your life, and your vision to everyone you meet (or who encounters your brand).

If your brand is a tangled mess of unclear concepts and uncertain associations, however, it's difficult for others to understand who you are and what you stand for. The 'stranger danger' sense is more likely to emerge if you are poorly or haphazardly branded, causing others to be wary of you, rather than accepting you as a known entity.

When we talk about branding, what tends to come to mind are major corporations like Coca-Cola, or pop stars like Lady Gaga. These are two fields that have leveraged branding strategies to capture and own large-scale concepts like 'family' and 'Christmas' and 'artsy' and 'fabulous.'

Most branding efforts, though, are far smaller and far more specific. Your brand is a smaller, far more manageable beast. And though it's still not easy to communicate, it doesn't require millions of dollars to leverage.

Your brand is an outline of *you*: your beliefs, your actions. The work you do is part of your brand, as are the clothes you wear and the type of computer you buy.

You have a brand whether you choose to acknowledge it or not: it's not so much a thing you build as a perception others have of you. That means if you put in some time to figure out who you are and what your brand currently communicates, you can make your brand 'speak' more clearly. Such tweaking allows you to decide which parts of your character you want to communicate first, allowing you to focus on what's most important to you, rather than the less-important bits that might otherwise overwhelm the things you really think are vital.

Let's say there's a skater (a skateboarder, not a figure-skater) who's fascinated by quantum physics. Science is a massively important part of his life, but that's not what many people will assume when they see him; the first impression strangers will have will more likely be something about his hair, baggy pants, tattoos, or some other obvious attribute that's actually less important to him than quantum physics.

Controlling your brand does not involve making things up about yourself, or telling stories that aren't true, but rather communicating authentic things about yourself in the right order and in the right way so that other people have the chance to learn the important stuff first, paving the way for you to add the secondary and tertiary characteristics later.

In the above example, the skater might have to tweak some elements of his look and presentation in order to be taken seriously as a physicist. He doesn't have to stop skating or even dressing the way he dresses, but in the community where he wants to be seen as a professional, he may need to present himself in such a way that his passion for science screams louder than his tats or skate wear. Why? Because if the first thing people notice about him is that he's a skater, that might also be the last thing anyone notices. If he can lead with the science, though, and follow up with the skating, then his tattoos and piercings are more likely to be seen as interesting character traits that supplement his main focus, rather than primary focuses unto themselves. His skater-associated traits, then, will help make him a richer, rounder person, rather than becoming liabilities to his craft.

Inventing falsehoods to support an invented image is often referred to as 'black hat branding.' An example of this would be if the aforementioned skater wasn't actually interested in science, and his supposed infatuation with it was something he fabricated to flesh out his brand, to stand out from the other skaters.

Avoid black hat branding. It may be easy to trick people into thinking you're something you're not for a while, but if you truly want to change the perception others have of you, it's best to *actually* change yourself. Don't try to force yourself to be what others want you to be, but become a better version of who you already are: a refined, authentic you.

I look at my personal brand as a personal recipe: a carefully curated blend of herbs and spices (characteristics and associations) that make up 'Colin Wright' as a person. Other people may use similar ingredients, but will end up with completely different flavors, textures, and presentations. Nobody is going to have exactly the same combinations as me, so my recipe is something personal and unique that I can refine and develop for the rest of my life.

It's worth taking the time to recognize and wrangle your brand so you can adjust and perfect it over time. If you examine your ingredients list and find yourself associated with something negative (in terms of the goals you want to accomplish, or your personal sense of morality), you have the freedom to extract or embrace that ingredient. Make sure you're doing it for the right reasons, but don't be afraid to try some wild combinations; you never know what will result from even subtle shifts in your combination of attributes.

If you never take stock of your own brand, chances are you'll never know whether the story you're telling about yourself is out of order, missing pieces, or a bad representation of who you actually are. Step back, take a look at what you're saying to the world, and adjust to taste. And continue to do so in the future, to avoid personal stagnation or misrepresentation.

LABELS

Labels are a double-edged sword worth wielding if you can make them work *for* you rather than against you.

Labels help us describe ourselves to the world in shorthand. Rather than going into all the minutia of our lives, our personalities, the specifics of our situations, we can point at something better known — a band, a brand, a celebrity — and say, "Yeah, I'm kind of like that." It doesn't capture everything about us, of course, but it helps others find the correct zip code, if not the exact address, of who we are.

The flip-side of this shorthand is that it lacks the wealth of specifics that make each of us unique. What's more, if we associate too closely with, say, a fashion trend or political party, we run the risk of sanding down facets of our personalities in order to better fit in. In other words, we might lose our incredibly important little personal details in an effort to be more closely associated with others who are similar to us.

This is the precarious power of labeling: it helps us connect with others more quickly, but at the risk of losing ourselves in the process.

I would argue that the risk is worth it, in most cases, and that the best way to negate the 'cookie-cutter' effect of tribes is to be comfortable living on the fringes of communities. Existing on the periphery of groups allows us to exist as human Venn diagrams: a series of overlapping circles, each one of them a label, but none of them individually covering the whole of a person. That central shape, which is different for each of us, is undefinable by any one circle, and expressed completely only by hundreds or thousands of them.

This approach is one of the better and easier ways to reap the benefits of labels without becoming a less rounded person for being associated with them.

The absolute best, though more difficult, way to deal with labels, however, is to become your own. If you express yourself clearly, create a movement worth following, and allow yourself to be unabashedly you, then your exact self becomes a label others can use as shorthand to tell the world about themselves. *You* become a zip code others use as part of their address.

Be brazenly yourself, even if that means living on the fringes of many groups, or creating your own to contain your unique collection of attributes. Use labels when they help you express yourself, but avoid being constrained by them.

WINNING

Life, for some, is a series of competitions. School, work, relationships: they can all be seen as an opportunity to shine brighter than those running the race alongside you.

Competition can be healthy, if you see it as a means of establishing a sense of self within a group, and use the actions of others to help stoke your own internal combustion engine. If your power source is fueled by that sort of thing, run those races and keep becoming a better version of yourself as a result.

There's another type of competition that isn't so valuable. The type that has us measuring ourselves against others and criticizing ourselves to try to spur development. In other words, rather than saying, "Oh hey, look what's possible! I bet I can do that, too," we might say, "They're better than me. I need to work harder so I don't suck so bad."

Negative reinforcement might be par for the course in the military and some corporate settings, but it's little more than self-flagellation when you act as your own drill sergeant. This approach is romanticized within some industries and endeavors (hard-core workout programs and entrepreneurship, for example), and it's a great way to wring performance out of yourself at the expense of long-term health. Mentally and physically, it's draining, and quite often in a very long-term way.

Consider that the presumed goal of competition is 'winning.' This term differs depending on the kind of competition you're engaged in, but allow me to propose something radical: winning usually isn't important.

If you're involved in a war or wrestling with an assailant, I'd say that coming out on top is a fairly sensible goal. But outside of a situation in which losing means dying or grave bodily harm, what does 'winning' mean, really? What does it actually do for you?

It allows you to feel superior to those you're competing against. It allows you to gain some kind of outside recognition, as well. A trophy. A title, perhaps.

But do you want to measure yourself by the standards of others? Do you want to live your life by a metric determined by those you're competing against?

It's like running a race. If you win, you outran the other competitors. So as the winner, you were the fastest of the group, and you gain a reputation for being the fastest among them.

The non-win-focused alternative to this scenario is running solo, or with a non-competitive group. I would argue that you're more likely to achieve the best you're capable of solo than when competing within a group, because you're trying to push to your own ceiling, not just be better than those around you. In other words, you can do better according to your own standards if you don't judge yourself according to the performance of people who have very different bodies, training regimens, and capabilities than you.

This allows you to compete in a 'you-sized' space. If I were to run a footrace against a bunch of kindergartners, I'd likely win. If I ran a footrace against a bunch of Olympic athletes, I'd definitely lose. If I ran alone, I wouldn't have other people as my metric of success. I wouldn't feel overcapable because I outpaced children, or incapable because I was left in the dust by professional runners.

What I'm left with is my own history, my own performance measurements over time. This allows me to grow incrementally, because rather than the standards changing with the performance of my peers, the only person I'm competing with is myself. And so long as I continue to grow, I'm winning. Always winning, always getting that burst of accomplishment. Every day a slightly better run time, and a slightly better version of myself.

So it's not that 'winning' is inherently bad or harmful, and some people *do* enjoy flogging themselves forward by comparing themselves to others, and don't mind that they may have to retire young as a result of that unbalanced approach to performance.

But if you're able to redefine winning on a personal level — to make it more about *your* growth and outpacing your past self — you'll progress at a far healthier pace. Competition will become less about beating the other guy and more about growing, together with anyone else who happens to be on the track with you.

It's amazing what happens when you stop looking at your peers as ever-changing metrics by which to gauge your own success — or even opponents to be defeated — and start seeing them as fellow travelers, pursuing similar goals as you, but doing so in such a way that their success doesn't mean your failure. It allows you to make far more friends, feel more secure in asking for help when you need it, and gives you the incentive to help others more frequently, as well.

Life isn't a zero-sum game; everyone can win. You just have to compete in a way that allows for it.

INSTINCTS

Trust your gut, we're told. That, or the opposite: think things through.

It's an unfortunate dichotomy, and a false one, because in many ways there are few things as informed as your gut, or as it's often called, your instincts.

Instincts are an evolutionary advantage. They allowed our ancestors to make lightning quick decisions about something without consciously realizing why they were deciding thusly. Instincts allowed them to see the shadow of a saber-toothed tiger and immediately freeze or run or pick up a sharp stick to defend themselves. Without knowing *why* they were jumping into defense mode, our ancestors would act upon information from their environment. Which is pretty cool, when you think about it.

This instinctual kick-start is still beneficial today. Instincts help to protect us from violence or theft, or when we find ourselves in an accident or some other non-standard and dangerous scenario. In the aftermath, survivors will often relate that they don't know why they did what they did; they just felt it was the right course of action. There's nothing mystical about such feelings; it's just a part of the brain that leaps into action when threats are perceived.

Of course, our perception of threats is based on data taken in throughout the course of our lives. What looks like a threat to me might look normal to you, and vice-versa. There's no universal 'threat' any more than there's a universal standard for 'good food.' Each person has a different palette for tastes and textures, and likewise, each person has a different collection of elements they see as threatening. And like food, our threat perception and threat tolerance is based on past experience, even if we can't remember having eaten a potato and choking on it as a toddler (resulting in a distaste for tubers), or seeing a violent crime committed by someone of a certain race as a baby (resulting in a latent distrust of people who look similar to that criminal later on in life).

Instincts, then, are evolutionary holdovers that still prove beneficial at times, but can also keep us confined. They cause us to feel unease around friendly people who are 'different' enough to warrant a kind of primeval internal alarm. Instincts cause us to worry over any kind of 'other,' because in our ancestor's time, 'different' often meant 'dangerous' in some way.

Being aware of this predilection, and feeding our brains more of what they need to operate optimally, helps us benefit from our instincts without falling prey to their overzealous or ill-informed moments. Knee-jerk reactions are guided by what we know and what we don't know, and the more we explore, learn, and experience, the more fine-tuned our instincts become. The more likely they are to be triggered by actual, legitimate dangers, rather than things that are unfamiliar but likely benign.

Trust your instincts, but not blindly.

RESPONSIBILITY

Responsibility is a tether. It's a connection to something that lives or dies without us, based on whether we're attentive or lazy; adept or inept.

Responsibility can also be an anchor, stabilizing your life and allowing you to enjoy the mellow waves as they wash harmlessly over you. It holds you in one place, yes, but hopefully in a place you want to be. A place that you care about sufficiently to dig deep, put down some roots, and become part of whatever ecosystem you've decided to invest in. Securing yourself in such a place can be magical, because it helps sustain you, just as you sustain it. Responsibilities, then, become a pleasure, rather than a burden.

That same anchor can feel like an iron ball attached to your ankle, however, if you want to be elsewhere. If you're not committed to one place over another, or if you don't care where you go, so long as it's not where you are now.

If you prefer novelty to security, and wings over anchors, responsibilities can be a horrible burden. They can be the bane of your existence; the only thing keeping you from pulling free and flying. They can be an unwanted gravity, holding you on firm ground, when all you want to do is drift away.

If there are people in your life, and if you are somehow connected to society — paying rent, eating food harvested by others — you can never completely exorcise responsibility from your life. You can alleviate its gravitational effects, though, by ensuring you take on only those duties and liabilities you can handle from where you want to be.

If you want to travel, you probably don't own a bunch of pets. If you want to stay put, you don't take a job that requires you to travel twenty days of each month.

There are responsibilities we inherit, through our families, our environments, and our pasts. There are those we have to figure out ways to carry more efficiently, and those we're better off figuring out ways to discard completely at some juncture.

Everything beyond that, though, we choose. We choose whether to accrue debt, whether to buy a house, whether to have a family, and whether to adopt a cat. We choose these things based on any number of variables, but often neglect how much they'll weigh on us; how much responsibility they'll bring into our lives, and what kind of commitment it will require we carry.

It's not your responsibility to want the life that others want for you, and it's not your responsibility to take on responsibilities that don't sync with how you want to live. Keep that in mind, and be very intentional about what burdens you decide to bear.

FLEXIBILITY

Strength is an excellent attribute to possess. It allows a person to apply energy to a task, move heavy objects, and survive through difficult situations.

When we picture strength, we often picture something solid, bulky, and immovable. I would argue that the truth is often quite different: strength is not just one shape or size, and is frequently more malleable than solid; quick rather than immovable.

Flexibility isn't something that's celebrated as frequently as brawn, but it tends to be the key to fortitude. Flexibility is the ability to adapt to changing conditions. It means you absorb the impact, rather than tensing up and bracing for it. It means that you bend when you need to bend, rather than locking your joints and going stubbornly rigid.

In essence, flexibility is strength that chooses resiliency over brittleness. Anything that cannot bend can eventually be broken, while something that is capable of being bendable, stretchy, and tensile can survive, so long as it continues to give under whatever pressure is applied to it. No cracks will form, because flexible means fluid and ever-changing.

It's strange that we worship brutish strength over a more

elegant, malleable variety, especially since nature prefers the latter. Darwin's quote on the matter is telling: "It is not the strongest of the species, nor the most intelligent that survives. It is the one that is the most adaptive to change."

In short, an impressive show of force can be helpful on the micro level, person to person. But in the macro, adaptability wins out. Flexibility allows a person to roll with the punches and change as the world changes. What's more, it allows them to apply what torque they *do* have to the places it will best serve. Rather than lobbing a boulder at every problem, the flexible person will hurl a series of small rocks at key points, or perhaps build some stronger weapon, if necessary.

Celebration of strength shouldn't focus on muscle (or the metaphorical equivalent) alone. Force can be valuable, too, but it's far less valuable without the flexibility to use it well, and to adapt its use over time.

AMBASSADORSHIP

We all serve as ambassadors for something, and in most cases we don't even realize it.

"Why do you use that brand of computer?" someone might ask. Or, "What's your city like?"

Whether you want the responsibility or not, you're an ambassador for everything you do, have done, and believe. This may not be your perception of yourself and your relationship to these things, but to someone who is not you, the specifics matter very little. As someone who knows more than they do about a particular topic, belief, place, or whatever else, you're the go-to person for expert information.

Remember that you needn't share anything with people who ask about your choices or history or anything else. You aren't a missionary, and if you opt out of proselytizing for whatever reason, you're still in the right. If you carry a set of moral beliefs and don't share them with others, you're not doing an injustice to those moral beliefs. If you use a certain brand of phone and fail to tell those who use a different brand about why they've chosen an inferior path, you're not failing to live up to the standards of your chosen brand.

But if you *do* choose to share, be careful how you

approach it. To be an ambassador is to be a representative for this thing you're championing, and that means your lifestyle, your actions, the words you use to describe it, all impact how everyone else sees this faith, product, or idea. If it's a religion you're sharing, *you* become an example of what people who follow this religion are like. If it's a brand of clothing you wear, *you* are now the type of person who wears that type of clothing — at least to the people who see you wearing it.

I feel this ambassadorship weighing on my shoulders when I travel outside the US, because I know anything I do may be interpreted as 'something an American did.' Not just an action that I took as an individual, but an example of some greater cultural trait; some 'American thing' that expresses a more expansive norm.

Consequently, I go out of my way even more than usual to be kind and help people and be a good visitor wherever I end up. I like the idea that people might encounter me and extrapolate a larger impression — of my culture, my system of beliefs, of the brands I choose to associate myself with — in a good way. I hope people are better off for having met me, and as a result, might be more open to the things and people and ideas that I think are important.

This is not always possible, of course, but it's an excellent course of action for someone who takes their ambassadorship seriously, whatever they might be representing, consciously or otherwise.

It's important to note, too, especially if you walk an unconventional trail, or have blazed your own, people will sometimes want to have you as a guide. They'll hope that, beyond just representing something, you might point them in the right direction, and help them navigate a trail you've created, or guide them down a path you've already walked.

Again, you don't *have* to share anything. You can live your life and allow others to live theirs, unencumbered by active ambassadorship.

But if you do choose to help others along the way when they ask for such help, it can be immensely valuable for everyone involved. The interaction will be valuable for you, because you'll live in a world in which more people understand your perspective, and it will be valuable for them because they may be able to go further, faster, as a result of your assistance.

RANGES

Life is made up of ceilings and floors, though not in the architectural sense.

Ceilings and floors, in this context, are the maximum and minimum potentials of something. The highest or lowest you can possibly jump, for example, or the maximum or minimum capability of a nation's economy.

Everything is a spectrum, and that spectrum is traversed by adjusting variables. These variables which can be adjusted are different in each and every case.

If you want to jump higher, you exercise your legs and eat a healthy diet. You might train daily, jumping and jumping and jumping, to get better at the motion required to achieve greater altitude over time.

A government that wants to produce more money can draft incentives for entrepreneurs and innovators, encouraging citizens to invent new things and build new businesses. A government can raise or lower taxes, pass laws that make people feel safer, and provide subsidies for key industries; whatever they think will result in better numbers on their spreadsheets at the end of the year.

All of these efforts are attempts to get closer to the ceiling;

to the maximum potential of which a person or group is capable. But the floor is there from the beginning. A person born with a certain weight, posture, muscle mass, and degree of balance can expect to jump a certain height without even trying. Any work they do from that point onward will push them higher.

Similarly, a governmental system will net a certain amount of tax revenue each year, even if they haven't enacted any new policies. Just by existing they attain a certain figure, and any efforts beyond that may help them push higher toward their potential ceiling.

Of course, ceilings and floors readjust over time. As a person grows older, for example, their ceiling and floor for jumping might change, because they themselves have changed. If a government opts for a different political system — democracy over socialism, authoritarian over monarchal — so, too, do their ceilings and floors recalibrate. The same efforts will result in different payouts, and what once worked (raising taxes, for example) may result in very different outcomes.

This is a useful metaphor because it allows us to see our limitations as spaces within which we can work — changing our position in the room we currently occupy — while also encouraging a periodic shift to different spaces altogether. It's possible to press up against the ceiling in one space, only to change rooms and find yourself somewhere in the middle, or back at the floor in your new environment. Whether this is a good change or not depends on where you want to be, vertically, and whether or not striving to move upward is worth the requisite effort.

Ceilings and floors are the latent endpoints for any skill or endeavor you might undertake. You don't get to decide where you start, but where you end up in relation to top and bottom is most definitely determined by you and your actions.

VIEWS

Views are temporal things, shaped by the *exact* perspective from which we perceive the world; a perspective that shifts every moment.

Views are not sacred. They shouldn't be, at least. To cling to a view because it's comfortable is lazy and all too common. This resistance to change is so widespread because there's a part of our brain that tells us 'familiar is better,' and therefore existing views take precedence over new views we might adopt — new perspectives from which we might see the world.

We're fighting against a massive amount of friction every time someone tells us about their views. Friction that exists because we mentally grapple with anything that seems novel or out of context, as a view delivered by someone other than ourselves will be, by definition.

But it's worth the effort, fighting against our internal safety-measures, in order to absorb, assess, and filter the views of others. What they have to share may be a puzzle piece that completes a picture we couldn't quite understand. What they have to share may be a perspective-shifting mind-punch that changes the way we see the world, and the people in it. What others have to share may change our priorities, our goals, and our actions.

Or it may not. It's important to filter because quite often the views others have to share are just as specific to them as ours generally are to us. My views have been very precisely honed and chiseled by my life experiences, and no matter how clear and beautiful someone else's views might be, they're tailored to a different individual. They very likely wouldn't fit me and my life any more than my views would fit theirs.

This is why it's important to respect the views of others while also giving yourself permission to explore and investigate alternative views without feeling you must change your own.

If you can find middle ground — touch-points you share with others that bridge your views — use it to grow closer and share what you can. If someone else offers up a perspective that blows your mind and changes your worldview, see what else they might be able to share; maybe there's a lot more they can teach you.

And if you find yourself influencing others, be responsible about it, and make sure they know that your point of view is just one of billions, and though you're happy to give them what insight you can, they should take what makes sense and leave the rest on the table.

The ideal is that we all share information, insight, and inspiration from our different views, making the world a rounder place for everyone. And hopefully we can do so without accidentally flattening the world by causing too many people to look at things from exactly the same standpoint.

THE MOMENT

Living in the present allows you to fully enjoy and understand the world as it exists *now*. It gives you an almost superhuman ability to absorb information provided by the world around you, and helps you perceive things you might otherwise miss.

When we're not in the moment, it's generally the past or future that dominate our thoughts.

When we focus on the past, we relive experiences that have already occurred and revisit places we've been. We indulge in flights of fancy about how we might have done things differently, or reminisce about how things happened, examining the details through the filters of our memories, with some elements emphasized over others, some details fuzzier because of their perceived importance or lack of importance.

When we focus on the future, we're plotting, planning, and hoping our way toward an idea of how things could be. We're wondering how we might respond to certain stimuli, or dreaming about an idealized sequence of events that will take us where we want to go. We are, in essence, planning our next 'now,' though there may be many 'now's before then, and many more still to come after that moment has passed.

It's valuable to be in the present whenever possible, but

reliving the past and theorizing about the future can also be valuable, especially if you're able to do it intentionally.

You can't change what has happened, but you can learn from your mistakes. Regret is a purposeless exercise, but respecting how far you've come can help you feel more confident about where you are now.

It's impossible to know what will happen next, but you can play out possibilities and determine what you might do should different potentialities arise. It's best not to over-prepare and leave yourself unable to adjust trajectories on the fly, but having some broad frameworks in place can help free up gray matter for experiencing the present as it happens, while also helping you feel more optimistic about where you're headed.

The past, present, and future can work incredibly well together, so long as we keep in mind how they impact each other, and what role each plays in how we experience the world. Make use of these timeframes as it makes sense, and avoid focusing on any one of them at the expense of the others, if you want to get the most out of all three.

REFINEMENT

In many trades and schools of thought, innovation is everything. The chief purpose behind most innovative efforts becomes disruption, upset, and upending established methods, implementing new, hopefully more effective and efficient means of doing whatever.

It's true that innovation and creativity are vital if you hope to evolve a craft or industry. But the under-appreciated practice of refinement is what carries us between eureka-moments, slowly but surely improving the world, and saving us from the changes that aren't all we hoped they'd be.

Refinment is, of course, an incredibly straightforward concept, and this is partly why people don't pay it due respect. The procedure is simple: learn to do something, and then do it over and over again, incrementally improving over time.

When you repeat a process many times, you slowly grow more proficient at each step. When French pressing coffee, for example, you open a bag of beans, grind them, pour the ground coffee into a container, mix it with hot water, press a strainer into the container to move the coffee grounds to the bottom, and pour the coffee into a cup.

Simple, right? A fairly uncomplicated process.

But even within such a rudimentary undertaking, there's room for incremental improvement. You might learn that a coarser grind for the beans works much better than the finer grind you've been using. You might discover that allowing the coffee and hot water to sit for a few minutes works better than filtering immediately, or waiting for five minutes. You may figure out that slowly filtering the coffee from the grounds works better than pressing it quickly.

Over time, the process is refined, resulting in better coffee. Rather than swapping in new equipment or some new set of instructions, the use of the existing equipment and techniques are refined iteratively, over time becoming more valuable for no other reason than you've done it a lot and worked out how to perform the motions more optimally.

Iterations often result in larger innovations over time, as well. Your expert use of a French press may help you figure out what it is about the process that makes the resulting coffee taste good, which could allow you to invent new equipment for making even better (or faster, or cheaper) coffee.

But refinement through repetition is key nonetheless, because without it, you don't know what to innovate, or how. And that new invention of yours will be rudimentary at first, and will itself require refinement to inch closer and closer to perfection.

Developing the ability to do the same thing over and over is time well spent. Repetition helps you improve existing skills, while also building toward innovative leaps. The value of being able to consciously and expertly repeat the same steps, the same exercises, and the same processes recurrently when warranted cannot be overstated.

VALUE

Goals can be difficult to accomplish. This is partially because they tend to be things that we have to strive to achieve, but also because it's not always clear *exactly* what we want. Maybe it's success of some flavor or another? Recognition, perhaps? Change?

Whatever the case may be, producing value, either as a byproduct or main focus, is an excellent guideline to adhere to along the way toward achieving your goals.

Consider that producing value helps you get where you want to be. By helping other people — giving them something they need — you slowly build yourself a cheering section; an audience of people who want to see you succeed, because you've already helped them in some way. This value needn't be given away for free, but if it's made available to the people who need it, and made accessible enough that they can make use of it, not just know of it, you've increased the momentum behind your pursuit of your goals. If you need resources, connections, or even just a helping hand from time to time, you have a much better shot of finding it when you've produced something that's improved someone else's life.

Consider, too, that producing value inherently leads to the

production of an asset of some kind. Whether this asset is a tangible product, a body of work, a word of advice, a reputation, or a movement to which others can hitch their wagon, you've built something valuable that you can later reinvest in, potentially making it even more valuable over time. If you can create such things as the fruits or byproducts of your efforts, you'll continue to move toward your primary goal (even if you don't know what it is yet), while also improving your own holdings.

Focusing on producing value in everything you do serves as consistency when all other options in the entire world are open to you. You can head in any direction, and pursue any future you want, and though you may pivot many times between 'here' and 'there,' maintaining a focus on value will ensure that no wrong turn is wasted time, and no goal is so nebulous that it's completely untethered.

Even if you sometimes fail to achieve other, more specific goals, you and everyone who receives the value you create will be better off for the effort you exerted and the time you spent.

SOCIAL QUOTIENT

It's tempting to draw a line down the middle of humanity and say that everyone on one side is an introvert, and everyone on the other side is an extrovert, but that would be a ridiculous oversimplification.

It would ignore, for example, that most of us aren't completely one or the other. It's difficult to find a pure introvert or pure extrovert because we tend to drift from place to place on that spectrum, depending on numerous variables, including the amount of 'me-time' we've had and the amount of socializing we've been doing.

It's important, though, to understand what range of this spectrum we tend to occupy; to take some time to figure out at what point we start to shut down in social situations, and about how long after that we'll need to lock the door and read a book, listen to music, or do nothing at all, so long as we're alone. Or on the flip side, it's valuable to discover how long we can stand to be cooped up without stimulating conversation or contact with another human being.

Here's an inexact metaphor to consider:

We all have batteries that determine how much energy we've got; energy that allows us to be productive, conscious, thinking people. Extroverts charge their batteries by being around people, and lose charge when they're alone. Introverts charge their batteries by being in their own heads, or indulging in individual activities; their batteries are drained when in public, in conversation, and when interacting with others in general.

This illustrates how a person can enjoy socializing, but still be drained by it. It's imperfect, though, because it implies that each person can only possess one type of battery or the other, which isn't the case. It's completely possible that you could be drained by people at work, and fueled by family and friends at home (or vice-versa). It's also possible that you could go months operating like an introvert, only to have a few week's worth of extrovert energy, due to the weather, your health, or any number of other obvious or obscure variables.

It's worth noting, too, that there are advantages and disadvantages to both modes of operation. Someone who is more introverted tends to be more inclined toward quiet, consistent focus, and often tries to create a controllable environment in which to operate independent of anyone else. An extrovert tends to make more and potentially stronger connections with others, and has an easier time collaborating as a result.

On the other hand, an introvert may miss out on opportunities catalyzed by those around them, and the benefits of working within a community. An extrovert may have trouble focusing in isolation, making projects without constant collaborators difficult to complete.

If you can take a measurement of how you tend to operate, and how much fuel from each side of the spectrum you need — your social quotient — you can create a lifestyle that never leaves you completely drained, and which allows you to enjoy the advantages of both introversion and extroversion.

DARKNESS

Inside each and every one of us is the potential to do some amazing things. But alongside that noble potential there's something else entirely.

Maybe you have the tendency to snap at professional inferiors, or sometimes take quiet joy in the misery of others. Perhaps you have a taste for victory at *any* cost, or a penchant for psychological abuse.

Whether your dark side expresses itself as a mean sort of cunning or an unfortunate reflex or habit, addressing this darker side of ourselves can be beneficial on several levels.

By being aware and conscious of this facet of your personality, you're more capable of staunching the flow of non-beneficial aspects of who you are and what you do. Like nail-biting or whistling to fill the spaces between conversation, you may be doing something annoying or harmful that isn't apparent until you stop and reflect upon the event afterward. Only then can you decide what behaviors can stay and what must go, and only then can you figure out a way to curb your aggression or dark moods or whatever else is manifested by this side of you.

Those around you will also benefit, as they may no longer find themselves targets of your negative reflexes or outbursts.

This can be advantageous professionally and interpersonally, and may result in stronger relationships and fewer tense interactions with those who might otherwise fear and avoid you.

Finally, by having greater control over both your positive *and* negative traits, you'll have a rounder mental picture of who you are, where you are, and where you want to be. You'll have a much better idea of what internal resources you bring to bear, which can help you accomplish your goals, solve problems that arise, and produce value for you and others along the way.

You will, in essence, be more complete, and though part of your personality is darker then what others typically see, knowing that you've taken this variable into account means you won't be caught by surprise when things take a self-instigated turn, or when a trigger emerges and you find yourself drifting toward your darkness.

Reach deep and acknowledge the dark parts of who you are, then sand smooth or sharpen those aspects of yourself, just as you would with any bad habit or misfit trait. It seldom serves us to conceal any part of ourselves, especially *from* ourselves. Accept that this darkness is part of who you are, figure out where you want to be, and act accordingly.

YOU FIRST

When entering into relationships, we have a tendency to bend. We bend closer to one another, because regardless of what type of relationship it might be — romantic, business, friendship — there's a reason you're bringing that other person into your life, and that means the load is easier to carry if you carry it together, both bending toward the center.

I picture people in relationships as two trees, leaning toward one another. Over time, as the relationship solidifies, you both become more comfortable bending, and as such bend farther, eventually resting trunk to trunk. You support each other and are stronger because of the shared strength of your root system and entwined branches. Double-tree power!

But there's a flaw in this mode of operation. Once you've spent some time leaning on someone else, if they disappear — because of a breakup, a business upset, a death, a move, an argument — you're all that's left, and far weaker than when you started. You're a tree leaning sideways; the second foundation that once supported you is…gone.

This is a big part of why the ending of particularly strong relationships can be so disruptive. When your support system presupposes two trunks — two people bearing the load, and divvying up the responsibilities; coping with the strong winds and hailstorms of life — it can be shocking and uncomfortable and incredibly difficult to function as an individual again; to be just a solitary tree, alone in the world, dealing with it all on your own.

A lone tree needn't be lonely, though. It's most ideal, in fact, to grow tall and strong, straight up, with many branches.

The strength of your trunk — your character, your professional life, your health, your sense of self — will help you cope with anything the world can throw at you, while your branches — your myriad interests, relationships, and experiences — will allow you to reach out to other trees who are likewise growing up toward the sky, rather than leaning and becoming co-dependent.

Relationships of this sort, between two equally strong, independent people, tend to outlast even the most intertwined co-dependencies. Why? Because neither person worries that their world will collapse if the other disappears. It's a relationship based on the connections between two people, not co-dependence.

Being a strong individual *first* alleviates a great deal of jealousy, suspicion, and our innate desire to capture or cage someone else for our own benefit. Rather than worrying that our lives will end if that other person disappears, we know that they're in our lives because they want to be; their lives won't end if we're not there, either.

Two trees growing tall and strong, their branches intertwined, is a far sturdier image than two trees bent and twisted, tying themselves into uncomfortable knots to wrap around one another, desperately trying to prevent the other from leaving.

You can choose which type of tree to be, and there's nothing inherently wrong with either model; we all have different wants, needs, and priorities. But if you're aiming for sturdier, more resilient relationships, it's a safe bet that you'll have better options and less drama if you focus on yourself and your own growth, first. Then reach out and connect with others who are doing the same.

FASHION & STYLE

There are those who take great pleasure in dressing so far on the edge of fashion that you might wonder if they accidentally stepped across the line. And then there are the rest of us.

I have no advice to offer the former — fashionistas and fashionistos — because they're far more fabulous than I could ever claim to be.

I do have a few ideas for everyone else to consider, however; ideas that have allowed me to blend into most social settings I've encountered, while also wearing clothes that accommodate my lifestyle and sense of aesthetics.

Consider that there's a difference between 'fashion' and 'style.'

Fashion is trend-based and determined by a combination of critics, insiders, designers, and marketers. What's 'in' each season is established ahead of time, and the consumers of fashion tend to be influenced by this process, while also (somewhat) influencing it in return; a fashion feedback loop. And it's no coincidence that as marketing has become a larger part of defining trends, new seasons have been released with greater frequency, resulting in greater sales.

Style, on the other hand, is defined by the individual. It can be influenced by fashion, certainly, but at the end of the day, my style will be different from your style, even if we wear the same brands. The way we wear things, the items we select, even the sizing is defined by the aesthetic sensibilities — the sense of style — of the person wearing the clothing.

Defining what attributes you prefer in the clothing you wear is a good investment of time, because you may be able to get the same bang for less buck by buying different brands that focus on the elements you care about. You may also find that some of the clothes you're wearing aren't as ideal as you'd like, and you can feel better about your personal aesthetics if you refocus your wardrobe on elements that are more *you* and less 'fashionable.'

Consider, too, that less can very much be more when it comes to how you dress. Buying fewer, nicer articles of clothing will usually result in fewer expenses and more satisfaction with your wardrobe, because you'll have more money to spend on those things that are most important to you. What's more, you won't spend so much time frantically trying to figure out what to wear each morning; anything you put on will be awesome.

Don't know what you like? A good starting point is to buy clothes that are well made, and clothes that fit, even if you have to spend a little money to have them tailored. Fewer brands focus on these two elements, because trend is more profitable. Find those that do, though, and you'll likely be happier with your clothing, and for a longer period of time.

In short: fashion is temporary, but style is forever. Develop a strong sense of style and invest in clothing that you like, rather than reflexively pulling out your wallet every time something new hits the racks.

UNDECORATED

How would you feel if you found yourself naked, not just of clothing, but of all accoutrements? No hair product, no makeup, no bracelets or rings or colorful socks? How would you feel without your waxed mustache, without your piercings, without your ever-present accessory of choice?

It's kind of difficult to fathom, isn't it? Even when we're naked in the clothing sense, we often have something else 'on,' whether on our skin or in our hair or whatnot. Something we feel helps us look a little more put together.

What I mean when I ask the question above is: how would you feel if you were completely undecorated? Hair a mess, face untouched by creams or powders, your body just as it *is*, not as it is when augmented?

Consider what it might be like — as a baseline — to be comfortable with yourself and *just* yourself. The unaltered you that would stare back in the mirror under the aforementioned circumstances.

Consider the power you'd have, should you reach that stage. You'd have the choice to use or not use the products that currently seem so essential. The ability to take your look, your vibe, in wildly different directions, because you wouldn't have one setting that 'works,' which you then cling to like a life raft.

We don't have to be supermodels to feel good about ourselves. In fact, one of the better ways to achieve a high level of comfort and confidence is to simply start working toward *something*. Clear skin, weight loss, more muscle mass, healthier fingernails; anything at all. Any pain-points that cause you to cringe when you see them in the mirror can be improved upon over time, with a bit of effort.

Although, it's nice to be safe inside a layer of decorative armor, that protection also keeps us from recognizing what we might improve, and allows us to neglect making those improvements. But why ignore something that can be so positive for your sense of self? Why put off becoming the best possible version of yourself, when you could start enjoying the benefits now?

Anyone who tells you that you *need* decorations to be beautiful, whatever those decorations might be, is trying to sell you something. Learn to love yourself without any physical adornments and you'll be far more capable of figuring out what additions you *want* to make. What accessories will accentuate, rather than conceal, *you*.

PERFECTION

Perfection is a golden finish line that so many of us pursue, sometimes to great benefit, and sometimes to our own destruction.

This duality of the pursuit of perfection — bringer of both growth and pain — can be confusing.

On one hand, we aspire to do the things we care about in the most ideal way we possibly can. This means continuous forward motion, non-stop repetition, and iterative improvements, punctuated by periodic leaps of innovative craftsmanship and learning.

On the other hand, the pursuit of perfection can keep us from enjoying and completing excellent work. We could get something to 99% of its potential perfection and still not be happy, because that last 1% still eludes us. What's worse, in many cases the author of a 99% perfect book, or the builder of a 99% perfect car may never deliver the results of their labors because it isn't 100% perfect. When you crave perfection, nothing else will do, and 99% is an embarrassment, though it may also be the best book ever written or best car ever built.

The trick to coping with the fact that you give a damn — which is why you aspire to perfection, by the way — is to remind yourself that perfection is an ever-moving finish line. That is, the definition of perfect changes as you change, as your craft changes, and as your capabilities change. If you write a book today, and really work hard to craft the finest book possible, you can only ever write the most perfect book you're capable of *right now*.

Tomorrow, however, that standard will have already changed. And the next day, it will have changed again. As your context changes, so does the carrot you're chasing. That means all you can ever hope for, if you *do* intend to publish your book or manufacture your car, is to produce and polish up to a point where the product will be valuable to those who might consume (or buy, or be inspired by) it. You accept that this is the most ideal you can muster in this moment, but the next thing you create will be even better as a result of your current effort.

The stopping point will look different for everyone, of course, because it's as much a comfort level thing as a practical one. There's no hard, set metric that will tell you when it's time to deliver your near-perfect project — to stop working on it so you can move on to the next iteration — so it helps to set deadlines for yourself, at which point you can check in and decide whether to keep going or unveil your work and shift your focus to a new endeavor.

The key is to never lose sight of the fact that you will get better and better, and that by repeating the process of going from conception to creation, you'll get better *faster*.

If you sit and fine-tune one car for the rest of your life, you'll deliver a single car when you die, because that will be the logical end of your quest for perfection.

If you iterate over time, however, you'll not only produce far more cars and create far more value for far more people, you'll also grow more skillful in your craft all the faster for it: not just because of the increased resources from actually producing (and potentially selling) something, but because you've made complete cars, so now you know what to expect, beginning to end. You can refine your processes and have a better idea of when to stop, and how much time it will take to get to that point.

The quest for perfection is strengthened by knowing at what stage of imperfection your work is suitable for presentation. Knowing at which point you end one race and start a new one.

Allow the pursuit of perfection to propel you forward, not hold you back. There's nothing wrong with being a stickler for quality, but it becomes a problem if that hangup becomes an obsession, rather than a passion.

CONSEQUENCES

In almost every case, the consequences of failure are not as bad as we imagine them to be.

The consequences can be bad, certainly. It could be that we don't land a particular job, end up getting snubbed instead of getting a phone number, or it could be that we simply do less-perfect work than we would have hoped in the office or at school. But very seldom does failure have permanent repercussions.

Unless you allow it to, that is. Many of the negative consequences of an action tend to result not from outside forces, but from our own negative thinking. We torture and torment ourselves for not living up to an ideal we've put in place, and flog ourselves with that knowledge any time we consider stepping up again.

Where this cycle originates is hard to tell. It could be solidified in school, where not knowing an answer or performing sub-par in any instance can result in punishment or humiliation in front of peers. Or maybe the pattern is set in motion on the school yard, where standing out means facing a very public psychological pushback. Or maybe with parents? Or work? Or relationships? Or…?

It doesn't actually matter where our fear of consequences originates. What's important is acknowledging that it's there, and that obsessing over consequences that are not literally life-or-death can make us less effective people, not to mention incredibly unhappy.

Quitting this tendency — to over-estimate the importance of non-life-or-death consequences — allows you to focus on solutions, not problems. It means you can focus on performing well, not on what might happen if you don't. It means embracing failure as a step on the way to success, rather than an indication of your inferiority or inability.

Developing a realistic relationship with consequences allows you to enjoy more positive outcomes, because you won't be spending all your time and energy worrying over the possibility of failure.

REFLECTION

To fully understand yourself and the world around you, it helps to take the time to reflect, and to make it a regular part of your lifestyle.

This isn't a particularly contentious statement, but even when we know that stepping back and allowing ourselves to register and mull things over is a positive activity, it's easy to get distracted from the task. We tend to put off reflection, sometimes indefinitely, to focus on results-driven, measurable activities, instead.

But being more reflective allows us to glean more knowledge, more lessons, and more awareness from everything we do. It gives us the ability to become more effective over time, which is a massive advantage when investing ourselves in future results-driven activities.

There are two main types of reflection worth engaging in regularly: social-reflection and self-reflection.

Social-reflection is identifying who you are and how you operate within the context of society and social situations. It gives you the opportunity to challenge your own ideas by acknowledging and considering the ideas of others, allowing you to see yourself through their eyes; a very useful perspective, so long as you can view it without judging yourself harshly, or assuming their opinions are inherently superior or inferior to your own.

Self-reflection is best done alone, and involves examining your own thoughts, responses, weaknesses, and strengths. It's a personal deep-dive, with the intention of unraveling more of who you are and what you want from life; how you might achieve your goals and become a better version of yourself.

Neither type of reflection is better or worse than the other, and they tend to work most ideally in tandem. Taking time from our day or week to stop and notice how we're responding to things, and how the world is responding to us is one of the most practical things we can do for ourselves. By being more aware, we slowly become more capable of adjusting what we're capable of adjusting to better suit our needs, both in ourselves and in our environments.

ONE LIFE

Nothing pushes me forward like the knowledge that I'm going to die.

I don't mean that in a morbid way. On the contrary, I think this knowledge is quite refreshing. The pressure to build toward something rather than building to enjoy — rather than living to live — is reduced significantly by this realization. It frees us up to consider what's actually important, rather than what we're told is important (things like legacy, for example, or dynasty). It allows us to focus on the here and now, because there might not be anything beyond that.

I should mention that I fully intend to live as long as possible, though I have no idea if the technology to keep me going longer than the now-standard 80-100 years will exist in time for me to make use of it. So it's a safe bet not to plan on any longer than the current average, and to plan, instead, to spend the years I *do* have the best way possible.

'Best for me' will mean very different things than 'best for you,' or for anyone else. If I told you your house was on fire and you could only grab one thing on your way out, what you would save would likely be different from what I would save. This same premise applies to how the finite resource of time is spent. If you had an hour to live, what would you do with that time? If you had 80 years to live, what would you do with that time?

We could spend our entire lives trying to figure out the optimal use for the time we have, but I think the best approach is to always be pivoting and changing course: to be introspective enough to recognize when your needs change, and to be prepared to recalibrate your internal compass any time you detect that you might be happier and more fulfilled taking another course.

This doesn't mean you have to wait to identify some lifestyle ideal before you start moving, however. You should always be moving toward something, even if you find you're going in the wrong direction at some point.

The fear of accidentally working too hard to get someplace we don't want to be can be paralyzing, but it's an irrational fear. By walking anywhere, we get better at walking (which, metaphorically, means we get better at living life and pursuing goals), which in turn allows us to reach future destinations much faster while having more fun along the way. It's also worth mentioning that movement toward anything provides a larger number of outside influences and opportunities, which help us triangulate a more ideal path even faster. It's not until we've walked a rocky path that we discover we prefer paved roads, and it's not until focusing on work that we discover we prefer to focus on family (or vice-versa).

Come to terms with your own mortality and make the knowledge of your temporality work for you. Far from being a morbid thought, this recognition is one of the most liberating and practical perspectives we can possibly have.

PREPARATION

Being prepared — to have thought through what happens next, and to have come up with multiple acceptable paths before a problem becomes a problem — is a useful skill to hone.

For some of us, though preparation serves as a security blanket in an otherwise unpredictable and perilous world. Over-preparation tends to be a common crutch for deep-thinkers in particular. You don't want to be forced into making spur-of-the-moment decisions, so you plan a course of action and adhere to it as much as possible. This gives you the ability to mull over multiple solutions before settling on one.

The downside of this methodology is that it often results in an ever-increasing dependency on such plans, fencing off aspects of one's life that can't be easily prepared for, and making the future feel like a series of predestined pathways from which we cannot deviate.

In addition to self-instigated rigidity, we may also fall prey to so-called 'paralysis by analysis,' which means we spend so much time preparing and planning for every eventuality that we fail to ever act. We plan each step of the way so carefully that we never take the first step.

The most ideal solution to this desire for preparedness

(which leads to lifestyle inflexibility) is to plan in a far broader sense; to essentially be prepared for anything.

Rather than focusing on a specific problem or sequence of events, learn skills and seek out knowledge that will allow you to plan on the fly, and that will allow you to utilize a deep well of knowledge and reflexes. This will result in similar benefits to those found in a well-laid plan, along with the flexibility of just 'going with the flow.'

What this looks like in practice is treating self-improvement as a core objective, day-to-day. If you're healthy, strong, knowledgeable, sociable, and capable of coping with discomfort, there's little you can't handle. Fears, then, will be faced and then disappear. Why would you worry about something you know you can handle if you need to?

The end result is a world opened up to us and our ambitions. What horizon can't we conquer, as this type of person? What problem can't we solve? And all it requires is that we apply to ourselves the same care and dedication that we once reserved for plans, so that we might always be prepared, no matter what we find around the next corner.

OTHER SIDE

We all like being right. After all, it feels good having the correct answers to life's questions; possessing wisdom that others lack, whether because of your background, your efforts, or dumb luck.

But there's an element to arguments and debates that we often overlook, especially those of us who like being right. Unfortunately, in order to see this facet, we have to let go of our focus on winning the argument and refocus on gaining perspective, building bridges between ourselves and others, and ultimately, winning at life.

When you become embroiled in an argument, ask yourself this question: what do I gain by besting my opponent? What, in other words, do I gain by trouncing them and making them feel bad about their opinions?

Ask yourself, then, whether it might be better to 'lose,' in the sense that you don't belittle your opponent's ideas or point of view, and instead explain your ideas, listen to theirs, and then do your best to understand where they're coming from. Chances are there is some small thread connecting the way they see the world and the way you see the world. Can you find it? Can you find the humanity in your opponent? Doing so can be a far greater challenge than out-shouting or out-debating the other person, and offers real benefits, in contrast to the temporary ego-boost we get from feeling 'more right' than someone else.

Consider that there might be grains of truth in the other person's arguments, even if you are coming from a wildly different place than they are. Consider that belittling someone else's opinions is a great way to make them feel bad, but a terrible way to convince them of something. Consider that by reaching out and finding common ground, you're actually *more* likely to get someone else to consider your ideas in the same way. By building bridges, not walls, you're opening the doors for others to see the world from your perspective, just as you're attempting to do with theirs.

We're taught that it's good to be right, that we're superior if we have the answers, and that the person who 'wins' an argument has the better worldview. This, of course, is an incredibly silly and 'schoolyard-logic' way of looking at the world. It's a model that is a great fit for reality TV shouting matches, but a terrible fit for people hoping to both learn new things and expose others to what they know.

If you're hoping to make yourself feel big at the expense of others, improve your arguing and debating skills. If you're hoping to walk away from tense interactions a little wiser and having shown someone else your point of view, then learn to empathize and shift your perspective. Learn to 'lose' arguments gracefully, if you want everyone to win.

NICE

As a general rule, it pays to be confident, helpful, and nice.

Those first two items are fairly self-explanatory. If you're confident, you'll reap many rewards: the ability to make decisions, a sense that you can achieve the goals you set for yourself, and an increase in how attractive you seem to others. Likewise, being helpful means leading with value, and allows you to build connections while also displaying what you have to offer.

Being nice, though, is an attribute that's often dragged through the dirt. A person who is pleasant or agreeable, we're told, is not someone who can do what needs to be done. Nice people are wishy-washy pushovers; not the kind of people who can negotiate well or manage an office. Why respect someone that's *nice*?

This is a very flat perspective, bred into several generations of businesspeople, who frequently use it as an excuse to be jerks.

Being a nice person means you treat other people with the dignity they deserve as human beings. Being nice means you're polite and collected. It means you're a pleasure to be around because you don't belittle others or intentionally sow discord and discomfort.

Nice people don't act out or act on anger. They're not unnecessarily aggressive, and they are never demeaning.

Nice people are, in short, confident people who don't *need* to stomp around to make themselves feel powerful, or put others down to make themselves feel tall. Nice people can afford to be friendly because they know who they are and what they're capable of.

You support nice people and cheer them on. You don't tolerate nice people, you invite them out for drinks. You don't secretly hate nice people, you help them make connections that might be beneficial. Nice people attract other nice people, nice things, and opportunities. You know why? Because they're nice.

The opposite of a nice person is someone who's intolerably aggressive, angry, mean, or petty. We've all encountered mean people, and without exception wondered how it is they've managed to make it through life, navigating the world using disdain and petulance as their calling card, rather than a handshake or a hug.

Mean people will probably always be lurking about, but we needn't help them spread the creed of 'screw everyone but me.' Treat others as you want to be treated, and if there's someone in your life who has nothing but venom for you, consider how much better your life would be if they weren't in it.

We may not be able to rid the world of mean people, but we can certainly avoid having them in our lives in any meaningful way. Support nice people by being nice, and by pulling your support from those who are mean.

OPINIONS

It's natural for us to achieve a new perspective, decide that it's the greatest of all great things, and then dig in, entrenching ourselves until the world forces some new realization upon us.

Consider that our opinions are shaped by these events, and, although it feels good to have concrete views that we can reinforce over time, it's far more ideal to treat them like rental property than houses we've bought and paid off. Rather than occupying our opinions like life-long homes, we should always keep a bag packed and be ready to walk out the door.

I say this because an active, curious, growth-oriented person will be constantly coming into contact with new perspectives and opinions, and to build bulwarks around whichever one we currently hold is akin to refusing to learn anything new. It's essentially saying to the world and yourself, "I've found *the* answers, so good luck trying to convince me otherwise, suckers!"

This is not the right orientation toward growth and finding your best-fit perspectives. Far more ideal is to invite other opinions and perspectives into your life and always be kicking the tires on something new. Rather than focusing on defending your existing constructs, why not test them? If your opinions and beliefs are really as strong as you think they are, they can stand up to the scrutiny.

And if they don't? Then you can move on to something better, be it a way of living, a belief system, or an opinion about which restaurant has the best burger in town. Modifying or discarding worn out opinions is like kicking off an old pair of shoes and pulling on a new pair.

I think most people worry that if they change their opinion about something, they'll be construed as wishy-washy or a 'flip-flopper' (in the political parlance). Changing your opinions as new information becomes available is not a weakness, it's a strength. It means that to you, learning is more important than some silly show of saving face. It's ridiculous to cling to an outdated idea simply because you always have and don't want to start fresh with something new. It's difficult to change once you've spent so much time with *this* way of living, *this* belief system, the claim that *this* restaurant has the best burger, certainly, but such adjustments are necessary if you're actually looking for truth, not just trying to be right.

In order to grow as people, we have to be humble enough to accept a hand-up when it's offered, and that means discarding the feeling of weakness when we refresh our opinions. Having the flexibility to change our opinions when exposed to new evidence shows us to be authentic, versatile, forward-facing folks, who value truth over reputation.

FEEDBACK

Feedback is a feisty, unpredictable creature. It's the type of beast that can make our day or tear it to shreds, depending on whether it brings the gift of positivity and congratulations, or the punch in the gut of criticism and bile.

On one hand, we want feedback because it ostensibly helps us get better at whatever it is we're pursuing; our cooking, our essays, our spreadsheets at work. The right critique at the right moment can help us move that much closer to perfection, correcting a detail we would have missed, or altering our trajectory toward something more ideal for the goals we're pursuing.

Criticism can also be beneficial in a more obvious sense: a positive report of a job well done. When we receive rave reviews for something we've produced, it feels good. It's affirmation that we kick ass, just as we've always suspected.

On the flip side, there are negative reviews: criticisms from employers about our spreadsheets, or scribbled notes from our teachers on our essays, informing us that we're not using the correct sentence structure and that our spelling is horrible.

Negative feedback is what makes us fear *all* feedback; the chance that our critique might be a bad one can be almost intolerable, and many people choose to change professions, jobs, or crafts, simply because they can't take the stress of what those who consume their work (or grade it, or pay for it) might say.

There's a trick that can help you with this fear of negative criticism, thankfully. When a piece of feedback comes your way, ask yourself this question: who is this for?

The obvious answer — it's for you — isn't always the correct one. In many cases feedback is given because the person giving it wants to feel strong, and capable of divvying out hurt or staunchly held opinions. Sometimes the critic had a bad day, and you were the unfortunate target they chose upon which to subconsciously let off some steam. Sometimes it's none of that: sometimes people just like criticizing others because they get a kick out of it.

Sometimes feedback isn't for you or the feedback-provider: it's for some third party. Maybe a review of your new book is written on a blog somewhere, and the author of said review wrote the piece more for their audience (who collectively love brutal reviews) than anyone else. Or maybe a teacher needs to be seen as strict, and as a result gives sterner feedback on exams than is necessary.

If the feedback *is* for you, then you must determine whether it's actionable or trashable.

Actionable feedback is something that comes laden with genuinely useful advice. "The sentences in this book were very choppy, which made the reading experience quite jagged and uncomfortable." That's an example of feedback that may not be pleasant to hear, but is worthy of consideration. Are my sentences too choppy for the type of book I wrote? Maybe I should take a closer look at that, and decide whether to make changes as a result.

Trashable feedback, on the other hand, is the variety that is definitely for you, but not worth your attention because it contains nothing actionable. "Not a good book, terrible writing." Note that maybe somewhere, someone gets their kicks by writing reviews like this, but assuming it's actually intended for you and not written for the thrill of putting down someone else's efforts, there's still nothing useful in there for you to work with, so you needn't bother with this type of feedback.

By asking yourself whether criticism is actionable or trashable, and filtering it accordingly, you'll be far more capable of coping with feedback, both good and bad. This process will also help you deal with the negative criticism without tossing it wholesale, which would ruin your chances of attaining real, actionable perspective and advice.

Just like you sort your mail, sort your reviews into valuable and junk piles. Then mull over the valuable pieces, and discard the junk.

DEFINITION

As humans, we want everything to be sorted and labeled. It's how our brains work: if we can't be reductionist about something, then we have to expend energy thinking hard about it and turn our conscious attention away from something more important, like internet cats.

As a result, we're fond of lumping people into broad categories. This friend of ours is a sports guy. His friend? Also a sports guy. That gal from the office is a geek, and the boss is a total soccer mom.

The differences between these people and others of their supposed categorization dim as we think of them in these terms. Rather than identifying individual characteristics, we instead define them in terms of the category in which we've placed them. "He's a sports guy that likes wine." "She's a geek who parties." And so on.

This is a flawed system in many ways, but the problem I want to address is that in putting people into pre-marked bins, we're defining them to ourselves, to others, and eventually, maybe even to the people who we're labeling. Because each assumption we make and each explanation we give in relation to this larger categorization is a strike against a person being able to have a rounder, richer, multifaceted personality.

Most of us don't even realize we're doing this to people until we watch for it and catch ourselves. That guy's a picky eater, so when he tries something new, my eyes go wide and I comment on the fact that he *never* eats anything interesting. How wonderful for him! I might tell myself this is a statement of support, when it's actually boxing the poor guy in. Maybe he's been working hard to try new things, and I've just gone and put him back in the box he's been pre-assigned to. It's an unintentional thing, but such automatic categorization can still have a major impact on how people operate and self-identify.

The best way to deal with this tendency is to avoid concretely defining others as much as possible. Rather than applying generic descriptors to people, allow them to be detailed characters, and avoid the temptation to push back when people who you assume are one way act another way. Maybe they have good reason for changing course. Maybe they're undergoing a major breakthrough and any feedback that could be perceived as critical, or any attempt to define them in a way that you're more comfortable with, could push them back down toward old patterns.

You wouldn't want other people to tell you who you are, or to describe you as a two-dimensional personality, so avoid doing the same to others. As a result, you'll likely have the opportunity to see and be part of more breakthroughs in other peoples' lives because they'll know you'll neither judge them nor intentionally or unintentionally make it harder for them to become better versions of themselves.

RESPONSES

You can't change the world around you. Not easily, at least.

And as a result, it's far better to have control over how you respond to the outside world, rather than trying to adjust and manipulate and manage every other person (and thing) on the planet.

This means that you decide whether or not to be annoyed by that crying baby in the seat behind you for the duration of your twelve hour overnight flight. Yes, your immediate, reflexive response may be to cringe and huff and sigh and moan, but what does that accomplish? Maybe you'll make the parents feel bad about something they have little or no control over? But more likely, you'll only make yourself more irritated and riled up. By reinforcing your annoyance, you ensure that you become more annoyed.

The same is true with things like jealousy and emotional pain. We all feel knee-jerk responses to things that happen to us or around us, but the responses we're handed by our brains aren't the ones we have to act upon. It's more productive to step back, analyze the situation, and then figure out which response makes the most sense on a practical level.

With the baby in a plane, you could be annoyed like your

brain tells you to be, or you could recognize that there's not much you can do about it and decide to be happy, despite the obnoxious crying.

Choosing how we respond to outside stimuli is an overlooked superpower we all have. We're told that we can't control anger and jealousy and annoyance and things that seem to rumble up from nowhere in response to the world beyond our control, but this couldn't be further from the truth.

Yes, it takes time and effort to gain control over these impulses, and yes, some people will have a harder time doing so than others. But is it out of our power to do so? No way. Many of us rein in our responses without even trying, on a case by case basis. All we have to do is harness that same 'logic leads to understanding, which leads to comfort with what's happening' process and make it our own, and repeat it enough that we jump into that analytical space right away, rather than defaulting to our animalistic reflexes.

We can't control the world around us, but we *can* control how we respond to it. Don't let that potential go to waste, and don't let life's little annoyances and pains ruin an otherwise wonderful day.

ATTRACTIVENESS

Looks aren't everything, but they are something.

Not just for the reasons you might think, though. The world just tends to go a little easier on folks who're attractive, even though 'attractive' can mean many things. 'The most-ideal, refined version of a person, given their base-line physical features' is a pretty good definition of 'attractiveness' for our purposes.

There have been studies done that show the average person trusts those who are more attractive over those who are not. People tend to care more about what the aesthetic elite have to say and are more likely to trust their word. We're also more likely to help attractive people if we can, even when there's no corollary to sex or relationships; just being decent-looking without any flirtation component is enough to turn the tides in the favor of a small sub-group of people.

Consider what that means for us and what we want in life; for the things we care about. If being a little better looking — dressing a little better and working out a little each day, perhaps — could help us spread the word about things we care about, could cause others to pay us greater mind, would it be worth the additional time spent working out each week? If we could be more convincing and capable of gaining assistance with building whatever we find ourselves wanting to build, would it be worth figuring out how to style our hair in a flattering way, maybe getting our teeth whitened? Figuring out which glasses suit the shape of our faces, and how much stubble is the right amount of stubble?

I don't think there's a clear answer for everyone. For some, the answer will be 'no,' because having to worry about all that stuff doesn't seem like a worthwhile tradeoff.

For others, the benefits may outweigh the time and effort spent trying to improve our looks just a little. This can be a tricky process, because we're taught that attractiveness is not something one should bother about overmuch, lest we be considered vain or self-obsessed.

But many people I know who have worked hard to improve their outer selves as well as their inner (myself included) have noted that the confidence boost and health benefits (of working out, in particular) enhance even further the results they see from their push to learn more, experience more, and get more out of life. In short, they feel their inside lives are accurately represented by their outside lives, because both are bringing them joy and helping them achieve what they want. The extra effort invested to be a little more attractive tears down barriers between them and their goals.

Again, there's no right or wrong way to view attractiveness and what role it might play in our lives, but for most people, making little changes here and there can add up to massive benefits over the course of several months or years. And though looks aren't, and *shouldn't* be everything, they absolutely can be something valuable if we have the motivation to make them so.

FOCUS

Minimalism is removing the unimportant from your life so that you have more time, energy, and resources to spend on the things that are important.

It's a powerful thing, focus. Minimalism is one way to achieve it. By removing the extraneous, you have a lot more of all the things you need in order to invest in the things that matter most to you.

But focus can also be about how you approach your work, your hobbies, your relationships, and anything else that's important to you.

Focus can be about monotasking: doing one thing at a time, and allowing your brain to process *everything* about what's happening with that one thing. Conversations become richer, work is easier, ideas present themselves with greater frequency and ease. This type of focus is momentary, but incredibly effective.

Focus can also be about goals. If I'm focused on becoming an Olympic athlete, I'm going to want to be in amazing shape. That means everything I do should somehow lead back to my larger goal. The food I eat, the exercise I participate in, the work I do; if the goal is important enough, and if I'm truly focusing on achieving it, most of the other aspects of my life should support my goal in some fashion, even if only in the tiniest way. Because enough of those little acts — enough running around the block and eating healthy meals — add up to something much bigger, over time.

Focus, in any facet of your life, allows you to put that which is most important to you at the forefront of your priorities.

But in order for focus to be a tool worth wielding, you'll need to know where you want to go and what you want to achieve. A full-out run is best utilized when you know which direction you're headed, so take the time to figure out who you are, where you want to be, and why you want to be there, before you start focusing on any one thing.

Also, be careful not to allow yourself to become a two-dimensional caricature of a human being as a result of too much focus. Moving toward a goal with that kind of intensity is wonderful, but allow yourself to come out of the zone sometimes, so that you can make sure you're still headed in the right direction, and are able to discover other passions worth focusing on along the way.

MORALITY

We all have a moral code, even if we don't call it that. Maybe we call it 'religion,' or a 'belief system,' or a 'philosophy.'

I call mine morality, because although there's plenty more to it than how to be moral (in the sense of being a good person), even those pieces lead back to what I think is right on a larger scale. What I think is the correct way to do things, and the right way to live, make up my morality.

Everyone's sense of morality is different, because everyone comes from a different place, with a different upbringing. Bajillions of different variables, both nature and nurture, make us who we are. And these variables impact not just who we are but also what we believe, and consequently, what we believe to be right and wrong within our conception of the world, humanity, civilization, and ourselves.

As such, I try not to prescribe any absolute moral ideas when I discuss such things — just considerations worth thinking about, adopting, adjusting to taste, or dismissing completely. Any of these options are fair, though I think it's important that a person know enough about their morality to know what to do with a concept to which they're introduced.

The best peace of mind you can possibly have is to be able to explain what you believe about a given subject, and to attribute that belief to yourself and no one else. "I believe this and that," and that's it. Not, "I believe this and that because my parents told me that's the way things are," and not, "I believe this and that because my religious leader told me I'll be punished if I don't." A rationally held belief is a beautiful thing, and taking the time to understand what you believe brings a sense of calm to your life that is nearly impossible to get any other way. That sense of calm is derived from knowing that you're acting morally, according to your standards; standards that you understand on a deep level.

Becoming more aware of what you believe — what your morality is made of — also helps you find gaps in your beliefs. There are many moral questions and quandaries that pop up over the course of a person's life, and knowing what you believe about as many things as possible can help you make the right choice when something unpredictable happens. Otherwise, you're left trying to do some serious soul searching, potentially with a very speedy deadline, and that's nowhere near the ideal conditions for asking yourself the deep questions and coming up with answers that best suit your ideology.

Look inward, look outward, and figure out what you believe. It will make your decisions far easier to make, your sense of moral unease disappear, and it will help you fill in the blanks of your belief system, making it far more likely that you'll make better choices more often, and face less regret as a result.

CONSIDERATE

Few of us take the time to consider, but that doesn't mean that we *can't* take that time.

There's no reason we can't independently address difficult questions and issues, and mull them over until we come up with answers that make sense to us, for us; or at least the version of us that we are right now.

There's no shortage of ways to spend our time. There are more activities and entertainments available than we could possibly enjoy over the course of many lifetimes. But even taking into account these many opportunity costs, it's still worth the investment to stop, question, analyze, mull over, and decide who you are, what you want, how you feel, and why.

Being considerate bears fruit: it allows you to know yourself and your beliefs and needs better, which makes the decisions you make and activities in which you partake more valuable as a result.

Let's continue to feel the weight of words and decisions. To compare, contrast, analyze over time, and look for all of the 'why's, so that we might better understand — and perform — the 'how's.

This is the end of the book, but viewed from another

perspective, it's really more of a beginning. What kind of beginning, though, is up to you.

ABOUT THE AUTHOR

Colin Wright is an author, entrepreneur, and full-time traveler. Colin was born in 1985 and lives in a new country every four months; the country is voted on by his readers. More info at asymmetrical.co/colin.

CONNECT WITH COLIN ONLINE

Blog
Exilelifestyle.com

Work
Colin.io

Twitter
Twitter.com/colinismyname

Facebook
Facebook.com/colinwright

Instagram
Instagram.com/colinismyname

Tumblr
Colinismyname.tumblr.com

ALSO BY COLIN WRIGHT

Dispatches
Exiles
Let's Know Things

Memoirs
My Exile Lifestyle
Iceland India Interstate

Nonfiction
Curation is Creation
Act Accordingly
Start a Freedom Business
How to Travel Full-Time
Networking Fundamentals
How to Be Remarkable
Personal Branding

A Tale of More Series
Trialogue, Rave Domino, Beige Man, Ink and Sand, Duplicitous Ox, Replicated Triplicate, Irresistible Blah, Stimulate the People, Volatile Frenemies, Masked Path

Real Powers Series
Real Powers: Part One, Real Powers: Part Two, Real Powers: Part Three

Ordo Series
Ordovician

Short Fiction Collections
Coffee with the Other Man
So This Is How I Go
Mean Universe
7 or 8 Ways to End the World
7 or 8 More Ways to End the World

Blog
Exile Lifestyle